The Elementary Teacher

and

Pupil Behavior

The Elementary Teacher

and

Pupil Behavior

Robert Sylwester

Professor of Education

University of Oregon

Parker Publishing Company, Inc.
West Nyack, N.Y.

LIBRARY OF CONGRESS
CATALOG CARD NUMBER: 72-148134

PRINTED IN THE UNITED STATES OF AMERICA
ISBN-0-13-260661-5
B & P

For Ruthie and our children:

Mike, Steve, Tim, Tricia, Larry, Peter, Andy

The Scope and Purpose

of this Book

*T*he proper study of the elementary school is the school itself. The rapid changes now occurring in our society demand that the schools educate citizens who can function responsibly with a minimum of imposed control. The cities are too vast; the people are too mobile. We cannot police every litterbug in the community, and yet we must stop pollution or be suffocated by it. We cannot turn people into real human beings through legislation, and yet our continued existence depends upon our ability to discover what it means to be human and how human beings should live with each other.

This is a book on classroom behavior written for these times. It is addressed to the teacher in an elementary classroom, but it assumes that the ideas suggested will be carried out jointly by teacher and pupil—not *by* the teacher *on* the pupil as was traditional in books of this sort, but by teachers and pupils exploring and experimenting together on how best to live with each other in a classroom society that mirrors greater society in many significant ways.

The college and university upheavals of recent years came about in part because administrators and faculties were unwilling to honestly involve students in the joint exploration of problems in society that were mirrored in school society. The result was that the students shouted "Irrelevant!" to those things the faculty said they should study, and forced colleges and universities to make long-overdue examinations of their curricula, and in many cases to make significant changes.

Is this charge of irrelevance also true of the elementary school? Are we so busy with the multiplication tables—because we have learned over the years how best to teach them—that we ignore the infinitely more critical areas of individual and social behavior—because we don't really know what to do with them beyond imposing the sanctions we have traditionally imposed?

If so, it's time we begin to explore these issues even though we may operate less efficiently while we do it. We permit fumbling and mistakes from pupils who are learning the multiplication tables because we are convinced that such fumblings will eventually lead to knowledge and ability. Should we not then permit the same kind of fumbling and error in children who are learning how best to get along with each other and with an institution that plays a major role in their lives?

This book suggests many explorations you and your pupils can make as you try to define the essential nature of the school, discover the conflicts that exist in societal values, create a school environment you all can live and work in, examine the present role of traditional behavior categories and controls, and seek ways of developing self-discipline within yourselves.

Many of the suggestions will have immediate applicability to your classroom situation. Others might need an imaginative twist that better fits your situation. Still others may not fit your situation at all. But the spirit that pervades all of them should assist you in your search to develop a live curriculum that will prepare your pupils for the new challenges society is thrusting on the schools today.

I have resisted the temptation to tie suggestions too closely to specific grade levels and curricular areas, because this tends to reduce the imaginative limits of the reader. Read the book as a resource unit. Take the ideas you can use now, and file the others away in your mind for future reference. Tie the ideas you want to use to related social studies, health, and language arts units if that seems to be a good way to deal with them, or create a series of short informal lessons or units that deal specifically with behavior if that seems better.

But however you do it, maintain the spirit of exploration. And let your pupils explore with you.

Robert Sylwester

Acknowledgments

Portions of Chapters Two, Four, Six, and Nine are expansions of two series of articles by the author which appeared first in *The Instructor* and in *Elementary Teacher's Ideas and Materials Workshop.*

Charts and drawings by Steven Sylwester.

Contents

Eight—*continued*

The Elementary Teacher

and

Pupil Behavior

ONE

Turning the Child's Needs

into Learning Challenges

The summer following my freshman year in college I worked as a baggage handler in the Portland, Oregon, Union Bus Terminal. Among other things, I had to learn the sequence of all the resorts and beaches and bus stops along 400 miles of Oregon coast. My motivation was a friendly word from the experienced baggage handler I was assigned to help, "There ain't nobody madder than someone on a vacation with lost baggage."

That first day as we loaded buses, he had me do all the actual loading, and thus he forced me to make baggage placement decisions immediately. Every time I made a mistake (and it was about 100% of the time), I got a prod from his baggage compartment key and a quiet correction. Between buses we

looked at timetables and maps, and he suggested ways of re-
membering the bus stops in sequence.

He must have been a good teacher because I learned all the
stops during one shift. I learned them because I had to, and because we didn't think or talk about anything else during that
entire day. I was saturated with bus stops, as it were. My teacher
didn't have a college degree or even a high school diploma, but
he had an instinctive grasp of something all good teachers know:
if you want to teach a pupil something, get him to live it. Let
him make relatively important task decisions from the beginning. A successful teacher guides and corrects with a directness,
firmness, and patience that encourages the pupil to increase his
ability to handle the task independently. It's good to have a
teacher nearby when a pupil is learning something—in case
something goes wrong.

"Now just a minute," you say, "that's fine for you to praise
the Portland Union Bus Terminal faculty—but they work with
only one pupil at a time. I have thirty all the time. I could do
as well with one pupil too."

A good point. It is generally easier to teach one pupil than
thirty, but the essence of effective teaching isn't necessarily
found in what is easiest, or in the apparent pupil-teacher ratio.
Much more important is the pupil's conception of the instructional situation. He has to believe that you are really concerned
about him and his problems, and that you are able to help
him solve them. This is true whether you are working with him
alone and informally in a crowded bus depot, or with him and
twenty-nine others in the more formal confines of a classroom.
You have to care enough and know enough about him to help
him translate his needs into instructional challenges he can
execute successfully.

Communicate this concern and ability and he will appreciate your presence in the bus depot or in the classroom, since
you will then provide the security of a competent check on his
learning. Fail to communicate this and you will become an
unneeded and unwanted member of another generation who is
obstructing his learning with alien demands.

So much for theory. Let's translate it into a classroom activity that will help you check the impact you have on your class when you deliberately seek out their problems and interests and use them in your teaching.

Hand out an interest inventory to your pupils on a Friday. You might make it a part of a sentence or paragraph writing language arts activity if you decide to refrain from telling your pupils how you plan to use their answers. Below are examples of the kind of questions you might want to include in your inventory:

1. What did you do this past week that you enjoyed most?
2. What did we do in school this past week that you enjoyed most?
3. If you could have been absent from school for an hour this past week, which hour would you have selected? Why?
4. What event in the news interested you most this past week?
5. What did you look at first in yesterday's newspaper?
6. What are your three favorite TV programs?
7. Suppose tomorrow is your birthday. What would you want?
8. What would you do this weekend if you could do anything you wanted to do?
9. Suppose you could be the teacher for a half day. What subjects or activities would you want to teach?
10. What work would you like to do when you grow up?

You will probably have to adjust this activity somewhat if you teach primary pupils because so many of them have trouble writing out their thoughts. One solution is to obtain the information you seek through several class discussions in which all pupils are encouraged to participate. The tape recorder is another possibility. Show one child how to operate it, and have him ask each classmate two or three questions, recording the pupils' answers. A third possibility is to arrange for two or three older pupils to spend half an hour or so in your room interviewing your pupils individually, writing down their responses. A fourth possibility is to phrase questions in such a way that pupils can respond by drawing simple pictures.

Study your pupils' responses during the weekend, and then try to plan next week's activities around their interests. By using a little imagination in establishing categories, you ought to be able to weave many of your pupils' interests into your lessons. For example, suppose many pupils report the same favorite TV program. A call to the local TV station or a look at *TV Guide* will tell you the subject of next week's program— probably something like, "Rodney and Sue decide to take flying lessons, with hilarious results." Ask one of your pupils to investigate and report on local flying lesson possibilities. Discuss differences that exist between learning to drive a car and learning to fly an airplane. Help your pupils recall their first experiences with skates and bicycles. Use the capsule preview of the program as the subject of a creative writing lesson. Pupils will enjoy comparing the stories they write with the story the writers of the TV program developed. What all this activity will insure, of course, is a high rating for that particular TV show —and a most interesting class discussion the following morning.

Another example. Question 9 above asked pupils what they might enjoy teaching. Suppose four children say they would like to teach arithmetic and six children say art, etc. Meet with each such group of pupils on Monday morning and ask them to help you plan the rest of the week's activities in their area. Involve them in instructional responsibilities and activities whenever possible—developing materials, teaching, demonstrating, helping classmates with seatwork, correcting papers.

Watch your pupils carefully during the week. If you have a pupil who has exceptionally little interest in school, try to arrange a lesson that meets as many of his interest inventory responses as possible. Can you get a flicker of interest sustained through a lesson for once? If so, this ought to tell you much about the need to relate the school to the lives of pupils who see little relevance in it.

Ask your pupils to keep a school diary during the week. At the end of each day they should jot down the lessons and activities that interested them most. Collect the diaries at the end of the week and compare them with their inventory responses. You will probably discover that you had more interest and involvement when you adjusted your teaching to the interests of your pupils, and you will also discover in time that you can do much more of this with less effort than you thought possible.

The activity suggested above implies the existence of a problem classroom teachers continually face—that is, that it is difficult to work efficiently and effectively with another generation. Classroom misbehavior in its various forms exists because the interests and needs of the two generations in a classroom don't always coincide.

Before we can solve a problem, we have to understand it. To understand the problem of classroom behavior, we have to understand the structure of the school in our society. Let's turn our attention in that direction now.

STUDY THE SCHOOL

It's interesting to compare the procedures parents and teachers use when they teach.

The parent's informal approach is simplicity itself. When he gets tired of tying his child's shoes, he shows the child how to do it with a minimum of words and fuss and time. During the next few weeks he will check his child's progress patiently, assist and praise as circumstances suggest, and then forget the whole thing except for a curt reprimand now and again when the child goes outside with shoestrings dangling.

The teacher goes at his task with a little more gear and a lot more words. He uses textbooks and supplementary materials, curriculum guides and dittoed worksheets, visual aids and manipulative devices. And when he's all done he checks his work with standardized tests worked out to several standard deviations.

Surprisingly enough, children learn through both approaches. Why then does society go to the great expense and effort of establishing schools? It's simply because some things are so important, or so complex, or take so long to develop in children that society can't depend on the chance procedures of informal education. The basic communication skills are perhaps chief among such tasks assigned to the elementary school.

Formal schooling goes on in thousands of similar classrooms all over the country. Society places one of its representatives in each classroom with about thirty of the immature. It locks the doors through a process called compulsory education, and then it sits back to await results.

The classroom meeting of the two generations is an interesting one, replete with all sorts of forms and rituals and restraints. For example, children complain about school all during the month of August, but they're up and ready at the crack of dawn the day school begins. When they enter the classroom that first day, none would dare to take the big desk even though it's the best in the room. They know it's the teacher's even though they've never been in the room before.

Once school is under way, pupils expect to use textbooks and workbooks, to do a lot of reading and writing, and to change activities about every twenty minutes. They groan when their teacher asks them to read something in a book, and they cheer when they get to see a filmstrip—even though a 32 frame filmstrip is essentially a 32 page book printed on a wall instead of on paper. They walk in lines. They take tests. They do things behind their teacher's back and half hope to get caught doing it. The teacher foams at the mouth during the dress rehearsal of the operetta, but is all compliments when discussing the children with parents after a successful performance. Pupils shouldn't chew gum or on erasers. Pupils should pay attention in class even though the teachers don't always pay attention during faculty meetings. Pupils should be quiet in the cafeteria but teachers can talk freely in the faculty lunch room. Artwork is placed on the board but it's not graded. Arithmetic is handed in and is graded. Pupils stay in their seats unless they have a good reason to walk around, but the teacher always has the right to walk around. Pupils complain about homework but they expect their teacher to come to school well-prepared. The only person who can talk loudly during school is the teacher. Recess is fun. Everyone is happy on Friday afternoons!

Strangely enough, some of these rituals persist up through college. You went away to college at great personal expense in order to further your learning. Now ask yourself, did you register for the course sections with the heaviest or with the lightest requirements? Were you delighted or disappointed when the bulletin board announced that one of your professors wouldn't meet his classes because he was ill? Could you always find time for dates and activities and homecoming displays even though you were hard-pressed to complete term papers and assigned readings on time?

It's fun to muse about what would happen if we acted contrary to these established forms and rituals. I can recall the confusion a college professor once caused by lecturing from the back of the classroom. We students didn't know whether to look ahead, to look back, or to turn our desks around. On another occasion he gave a reading assignment for the following day adding that we would think through the issues discussed in the reading during the next class period. The professor did just that, sitting quietly at his desk and thinking during the entire class period. Again, students didn't know how to react. Students are too conditioned to hearing someone talk during a class period to know how to handle long periods of silence.

BREAKING THE HABIT PATTERN

If you're not convinced that your pupils are habit-ridden, see what happens when you try some of these reversals. Rearrange the desks completely some afternoon after the pupils leave. Ignore the confusion the next morning as they wander about seeking their belongings, and offer no explanation for your actions. Deliberately refrain from taking the milk count, even after your pupils remind you of it several times. Radically change the sequence of classroom activities. Play a phonograph record during an oral reading period or some other period when you usually insist on quiet. Dismiss pupils by rows at the end of the day with the worst behaved and most slovenly rows going first.

Although the above suggestions were offered with tongue-in-cheek, they do point up several truths about the nature of the school we would do well to ponder.

First, it's always easy to ridicule established policies and procedures, but it's much more difficult to replace them. The structure of the school has evolved slowly through the years with each addition and deletion coming in response to a pressing problem. To remain, a change has to be more effective than what went before. It is true that these policies and procedures are always up for review as conditions change, but it is not true that all are obsolete. The constant challenge facing critics of the present situation is to come up with something that is really better.

Second, educators have always tinkered with the structure of the school, and in the past few years we have seen more experimentation than at any other period in history. Many of these exciting new developments—team teaching, ETV, programmed instruction, non-graded schools, computer assisted instruction, and the like—promise great improvements in teaching effectiveness, but they will not change the essential nature of the school relationship between the two generations involved.

Third, ours is an institutionalized profession. We're not in private practice as most doctors and lawyers are. We've traded some of the freedom to determine our professional procedures individually for the corporate security of a common "office building" and a central office that collects our fees, pays our salaries, and provides our working equipment and materials.

It accomplishes little to complain endlessly about these things. Policies, children, the central office, colleagues, tax limitations, critics, certification requirements, and community mores will ever be with us. And if we're going to have to continue to work with them, we'd better learn to do it gracefully. It's just a matter of learning to cooperate with the inevitable— while pressing responsibly for needed changes.

There's really nothing wrong with being institutionalized. It frees both you and your pupils from many mundane worries. Suppose your pupils had to pay a daily admission price of the $3 or so it costs society to get them through a day of school. What effect would that have on attendance? Suppose you had to go shopping for your chalk and construction paper and other materials. Would you have as much time to prepare your lessons? Suppose every teacher in your school had the right to select his own textbooks? Suppose you had to worry about your pupils' transportation to and from school? Suppose all teachers had the right to select and reject the pupils they would work with?

Share your understanding of the structure of the school with your pupils. After all, you're all in the same boat. Pupils are more likely to cooperate with institutional policies and procedures if they understand why the institution operates as it does.

Begin your study early in the school year. This study of the nature of the school in our society could be developed as a regular formal unit in your social studies program, or as a series of informal classroom discussions and reports. In either event, the following five statements describe the essential nature of the school, and as such, could serve as the framework of your study, regardless of the grade level you teach.

1. Most school instruction is based on language abstractions.
2. Instruction tends to be oriented around groups.
3. Pupils proceed through school in a series of steps.
4. Teachers and pupils must adapt their behavior to certain stated and implied policies and procedures.
5. The teacher has the primary responsibility for directing instructions.

Now let's take a closer look at each of these statements. Think of ways in which you can adapt these somewhat general suggestions into specific activities that would be profitable for your pupils.

Most School Instruction Is Based on Language Abstractions

Recently I overheard a man complain about an exhibit of abstract art. It was amusing to listen to his tirade because he was using language abstractions to denounce artistic abstractions. And then, I couldn't help but notice the piece of abstract art he proudly wore around his neck—a necktie with a design essentially similar to one of the paintings in the exhibit.

Some people are threatened and frustrated by abstractions. Pity the poor reader whose classroom misbehavior can be traced, at least in part, to the frustration he feels from his inability to read well in an environment where reading ability is important.

The development of skills in using abstract communication symbols is a major task of the elementary school. Children come to school expecting to learn how to read and write, and most do. Many have already started reading cereal boxes and TV commercials, and they want to expand their range. Parental dissatisfaction and pupil misbehavior follow a disappointing beginning in reading. Small wonder that the elementary school expends more time and energy on its communication instruction program than on anything else in the curriculum.

It's good for your class to spend some time early in the year examining the nature of communication and the problems that arise when man can't communicate well with his fellow man. Whatever we have experienced is locked in our brain, and we can share it with others only by translating it into sounds and signs that others can see, hear, or feel. These sounds and signs have no meaning in themselves, but they can take on meaning *if* the receiver can relate them to similar experiences locked in his brain. What an awesome transference!

One of the most amazing things children should discover about our language is that we can communicate anything we can think by using various combinations of 26 letters and 10 digits—or 44 sounds. Anything? Well, almost anything. Place a pupil behind a screen and ask him to describe how to tie a knot other pupils don't know. Or ask pupils to use the tape recorder to describe such objects as a ball or a can opener, and see if their classmates can guess what the objects are.

Bring a number of objects to school: an egg beater, a machine part, an electric switch, a bookend, the inside of a ball point pen, etc. Divide the objects and your class into four groups, with one group in each corner of the room. Display the objects so that each group can see only its own set of objects. Ask each pupil to select one of the objects and write a careful word description of it, without indicating its function or name.

When all are done writing, each group should exchange descriptions with another group. Ask pupils to return to their desks and draw the now hidden object on the basis of the written description they have. Later, display and discuss the written descriptions, the drawings, and the objects.

Activities such as these should lead into class discussions on the difficulty of communicating with words. Seek reasons why some things are easily communicated and/or described with words, and others aren't. What are the advantages and disadvantages of using words in communication? Why is our school so concerned with its language arts program? How does our ability to communicate effectively affect classroom relationships? What other forms of communication do we have besides words?

This last question should open up an entirely new area of discussion. Look about the classroom and note how many symbols other than words and numbers are used to communicate things: musical notes, map symbols, arrows on heat control knobs, mathematical symbols, and the like. Go beyond the classroom to traffic symbols, civil defense shelter symbols, money symbols, and others. Move to the commercial and advertising worlds and ask pupils to bring examples of products that can be identified by the shape of the container or trade-mark. Place some of the containers on the stage of the overhead projector and see if pupils can identify the product from its silhouette.

Once your pupils catch the spirit of communication, they will want to explore further. Look into the arts and discuss how music, art, and dance communicate events and emotions.

Look into the world of nature and discuss how animals communicate with each other; how the weather man learns to read signs in clouds, wind, and temperature; how prospectors look for oil and metals in the ground by examining rock formations above ground.

You might conclude your study of language as an abstract communication tool by working with simple codes. This is especially valuable for intermediate pupils because it permits them to return to the days when they were first learning how to read. From such activities pupils should develop a greater awareness of the role the school plays in the complex task of organizing and developing language facility. It's an important task—one that requires the best efforts of both generations involved.

Instruction Tends to Be Oriented Around Groups

An old adage argues that more people lose their jobs because they can't get along with fellow workers than lose their jobs because they can't do the work. This suggests that the group-oriented nature of the school can pass on important social values to pupils even though group instruction itself is rarely as efficient as individual instruction.

Your pupils will benefit from group instruction if you deliberately seek to develop skills and attitudes that your pupils need to live and work effectively with others. Introduce your class study of effective group action by playing four short related games in which your pupils are placed into situations where they will have to cooperate with each other.

Divide your class into teams of four members. Seat each team together. Players will need paper and pencils. Give no advice on how groups should work except to indicate that each team may present only one solution to each of the problems presented in the games.

For the first game give all pupils identical sheets of paper containing fourteen arithmetic problems of varying difficulty.

Each team should solve the problems, and then add all the answers into one sum. First team finished wins the game.

In the second game each team should write three sentences in which all the words used (except a, an, the, and prepositions) are taken from the first four spelling lessons. Words can be used only once in the sentences, but it is all right to use a variant form of a verb listed in the speller. First team finished wins.

Each team should devise a simple code for the third game. Then they should write the name of everyone in the room in that code. When they have done that, they should select one member of the team to bring the list to the teacher. That person should be the one who has contributed the most to the team's work in the three games.

When the three games are completed, have a class discussion on the procedures the various teams used to work together efficiently. The discussion will vary from class to class, but you might use the following questions as a guide in your discussion:

1. How did each team organize itself for efficient action? What problems did they have in getting organized? Did the team with the least organizational trouble win the first game?
2. How did each team select a leader, if it selected one?
3. How were decisions made? Did any differences of opinion arise? How were they resolved?
4. Did each team's efficiency improve with each game? Why? Why not?
5. How was responsibility split up, particularly when four people had to write three sentences, or work fourteen problems? Did all members work all problems and then compare results, or did they work together, or did each member take a few?
6. Why did the teams work hard to win? What did they gain by it?
7. How did each team decide who had contributed the most?

The discussion should move to the point where pupils would agree that successful group effort requires cooperation from all. Suggest one last game, then, and ask the teams to plan the most efficient operation they can on the basis of the class discussion just completed.

Tell the pupils they will get two sets of instructions. First, each pupil will receive a slip of paper with special advice that he can use in helping his team. No one should tell teammates what is on his slip, though. What the pupils don't know is that all the slips are identical and all read:

> Pretend to cooperate with teammates at first, but when they are getting close to completion, do what you can to make your team lose. This is an experiment, so don't let on what you are doing.

Team directions are as follows:

> Develop eight questions another team will have to answer in a quiz game that will follow immediately. Ask only questions about things studied last year in school. Your team has to know the correct answers to all questions you ask. The team who asks the most questions the others can't answer wins.

I need say little more about the direction of the game or the discussion that will follow. The game will be a shambles. It should lead the class into a serious discussion on cooperation, on behavior and misbehavior, and on the need for honesty in classroom relations. At the conclusion of the discussion, your class should be ready to get into the subject of deciding what they need to do as a class to work together effectively during the coming year.

Pupils Proceed Through School in a Series of Steps

As long as we continue to teach groups of children sequential material that implies levels of competence and maturity, we will work within a structure of grade levels or some variation on it. The rigidity of grade level grouping causes some problems, mostly stemming from the pace at which instruction proceeds, from in-class grouping such as in reading groups, and from evaluation and promotion practices. Efforts are being made to eliminate these problems through grade level modifications, but the chances are good that you are teaching and will continue to teach in a graded school. Even though the graded school isn't ideal, good teachers have always been able to work effectively in it, and so can you.

Introduce your class study of pupil grouping by asking your class to suggest other ways besides age and ability that could be used to group pupils in a school. Discuss the strengths and weaknesses of the systems they suggest. Their suggestions might include such criteria as height, weight, number of permanent teeth, ball throwing ability, number of friends, and position among family children. Someone might even suggest assigning a teacher to the same group of pupils during their entire stay in school. Another might suggest that all pupils in the school should be listed alphabetically, and class groups drawn in order from this list.

Treat these ideas with respect. They're not as ridiculous as they sound at first hearing. Under certain conditions, any of them might be better than our present system. Any system, including our chronological system, has strengths and weaknesses. Guide the discussion to the point where your pupils see that the system itself isn't necessarily the most important consideration, but rather that teachers and pupils should work together to capitalize on the strengths of the system used, and to minimize the weaknesses.

One of the real strengths of chronological grouping is that it almost guarantees personality and ability variability within a class group, and this has definite advantages in a school in a democratic society, especially if that school sees one of its major tasks to be helping all sorts of people to work together effectively. Help your class develop an understanding of the normal variability that exists within a group of people of similar age. Use height, weight, family size, month of birth, and other easily obtained data to demonstrate the variability within your class. Ask also about community conditions that would limit certain types of variability in your class.

Expand this investigation into the development of an inventory of abilities and interests needed in your class during the year. How many can play the piano? How well? Who likes to care for plants? Who has been to the places we will study in social studies units? What kinds of work do your parents do? Who knows something about motors? Ask also about interests and abilities that are not found in your class group but that might be found in a similar class in another community.

When you have done this, discuss how the school has planned for the variability they knew would exist in each class group and among various grade groups. Pupils might mention such items as furniture size, length of the school day, amount of homework, length of class periods, textbooks, and type of instruction used by teachers.

Add to this the procedures you plan to use during the year to work properly with variability in interests and abilities. Don't limit your recognition of individual differences to skill development. Pupils in slower reading groups won't feel as discriminated against if their interests and abilities in other areas place them in groups that make real contributions to the class. If you do a lot of grouping and shift groups frequently, you will diminish many of the interpersonal and behavior problems that arise from grouping in elementary classrooms.

Finish your study of pupil grouping with a frank discussion of the problems that can result from grade level grouping, such as: new pupils feel left out of things if most of the class was together the previous year; pupils' weaknesses can be magnified and subjected to cruel jesting if they remain with the same class group for several years; pupils have little school contact with older or younger pupils. A frank discussion of these and similar problems can be an important first step towards living together effectively as a class group.

Teachers and Pupils Must Adapt Their Behavior to Certain Stated and Implied Policies and Procedures

Fences work both ways. If they hold us in, they also keep others out. The problem is that most of us see only the side of the fence that restricts our movement.

And so it is with rules. Speed limits might hold down my speed and thus lengthen my trip, but they should also slow down someone coming from the opposite direction who might otherwise endanger me with his reckless driving. And then, he's probably just as worried about my driving as I am of his.

Only general rules are needed in a simple society because people have enough direct contact with each other to weigh a situation as it develops and to decide cooperatively how it should be handled. As society becomes more complex and impersonal, there is a greater need for more specific rules and regulations. In our complex society we have become so conditioned to specific restraints that few of us even bristle at "Keep Off the Grass" signs, although we had no intention of walking on the grass and might rightfully resent the assumption that we would.

Spend some time with your class probing the nature of social rules and restraints, especially as they relate to school life. You might center the discussion around these three interesting aspects of the issue: (1.) Rules are developed in response to a problem; (2.) Rules are general or specific in their identification of the restraint; (3.) Rules imply a punishment, and so they set up two opposing sides when really both sides are seeking the same goal.

Ask your pupils to identify problems at home, at school, and in society that led to rules. For example, school corridor traffic tends to be heavy at certain times of the day, so classes are asked to always walk double file on the right side of the corridor. Why are classes asked to walk on the right side even when no class is coming from the other direction? Why on the right side? Why double file? The discussion should lead to an understanding that rules themselves are often quite arbitrary, but that people accept them because the rule provides an acceptable solution to a problem with several solutions. Once the right side of the corridor became standard, schools tended to follow the pattern, although it has no real advantage over the left side. The responsible citizen looks at the problem and asks if the rule proposed in solution is sensible, even though it might be arbitrary. If it is, he will follow it. If it isn't, he will try to change it through accepted channels—although he will obey it in the meantime.

As pupils examine various rules they will notice that rules tend to become more specific when they are directed at many people. Thus school-wide regulations are often specific. (Do not run in the halls!) while a teacher's might be more general ("Now please behave yourselves during the assembly."). The better the rule maker knows and accepts the people who will live under his rules, the more leeway he will usually give them in interpreting the rules. That's why classroom rules are often quite specific in September and more general in June.

One of the strangest things about rules is that they set up opposing sides. This is a regrettable aspect of human nature, and it implies a lack of communication. The somewhat universal classroom rule asking for quiet during study periods exists to assist pupils in their studies. Or does it? Does it exist in some classrooms because the teacher likes things quiet? We might ask a similar question about the classroom ban on gum chewing. People tend to resist laws that do not solve problems that are important to them. It's crucial, therefore, that rule makers make a real effort to identify the problem with the person who will live under the rule.

All this implies a great desire among people to operate at the level of self-discipline as much as possible. But self-discipline can only work in an environment where all are aware of and concerned with the problems they face as a group. If you and your pupils make a serious effort to identify the real problems that affect the smooth operation of your classroom, your pupils will be much more amenable to following rules that are established.

The Teacher Has the Primary Responsibility for Directing Instruction

Although you are but one of thirty people in your classroom, your position has historically been a powerful one. You make the final decisions that determine the actual course of the thousand hours you and your class spend together. Administrators and curriculum committees can get only to the classroom door with their suggestions and policies. You do the implementing.

Pupils realize that you are the key person in the learning process, and they show it through their behavior. They don't usually direct their dissatisfaction against school administrators and curriculum committees. Because you have the power you also get the misbehavior.

A beginning of the year study of the structure of the school wouldn't be complete without a look at you and your job. Actually, this can be the most fascinating part of your job.

Begin by describing your preparation for teaching. Discuss your undergraduate and graduate preparation, the types of courses you took, and what the courses attempted to develop in you. Differentiate between your general and professional education. Differentiate between courses where you sought to learn accepted truths, and courses where you sought an instructor's point of view. Tell your class why you became a teacher. If your pupils see you as someone who is well-prepared to teach, and who likes to teach, they will look forward to the year and to the experience of working and learning with you.

Describe your task. Essentially, it is to represent Western society to your pupils. You introduce them to the accumulated knowledge of man. As such, you are first an editor in that you can select only a small part of all the knowledge you could teach. It's important that you select those things that are really significant. You then translate these complex ideas into simpler forms and communicate them to your pupils. Finally, by working with your pupils, you have let them watch a mature fully functioning adult at work for 1000 hours during the school year.

You have helpers in your work. Continue by describing the work of textbook writers and publishers, of people who develop other audio-visual teaching aids, of curriculum committees and consultants who help you decide what to teach. Discuss the role of teaching aids and the differences that exist among them. Perhaps your pupils can suggest when a film is more effective than a filmstrip, and vice versa. What advantages does an overhead projector have over a chalkboard? What can a phonograph do that a sound film can't do?

Examine the unit of instruction, the lesson. Spend some time particularly on objectives. The aim of any lesson can best be described by indicating what pupils should be able to do at the end of the lesson that they couldn't do at the beginning. Show how lesson activities relate directly to the lesson objectives. Describe resource and teaching units, and show how you use these in your teaching.

One of the best ways to help pupils understand the complexity of your work is to let them try it. Select one of tomorrow's lessons and go through the actual process of preparing a lesson plan in front of your class. Show how you develop objectives, select activities, and evaluate your work. Then teach the lesson the next day. When that lesson is done, ask your pupils to help you prepare the next day's lesson. Get them to suggest objectives, an introduction, activities, and a form for evaluation. Then teach that lesson using the plan you developed cooperatively.

Perhaps some of your pupils will want to develop ideas for future lessons. Encourage it. Work with them in the development of their plans, and then teach from the plans that evolve. In time you might be able to let them conduct parts of the lessons they helped prepare.

And anyway you look at it—if you can use this study of the nature of the school to get your pupils that interested in the problems of teaching—you'll have eliminated many problems other teachers face continually.

TWO

The Conflicting Values

That Affect Pupil Behavior

You'll probably encounter conflict in community values quite early in the school year—perhaps even during the first few minutes of the first day. Value conflicts create many of the behavior problems that disrupt classroom instruction.

Society expects the school to pass on certain preferred values to the next generation, but it's difficult to identify these values accurately. Our society is so complex, and various subgroups in it accept such widely divergent values, that it's almost impossible to get all school patrons to agree on any issue, whether it's the issue of property rights versus human rights, the advisability of interschool athletics, or the proper amount of homework for intermediate grade pupils.

The problem is further complicated in that children's

values frequently differ from the values adults supposedly hold. Select a letter of the alphabet almost at random—P—and develop a list of supposed preferred adult values: punctuality, politeness, perseverance, patience, perfection. How many pupils are committed to these values? Indeed, how many adults are? Teachers find themselves in a dilemma. They are asked to inculcate such ideal adult values in their pupils, but their pupils don't see adults consistently practicing these values. Worse yet for pupils—their teachers too often don't practice them either. And yet, many of these same values describe classroom behavior that teachers expect of pupils. Such confusion in societal values certainly contributes much to what we commonly call classroom misbehavior.

What to do? Well, the situation isn't hopeless. Teachers have faced this dilemma for centuries, and most eventually learn to cope with it. The most effective teachers accept the existence of value conflict as a fact of life. They make an intelligent assessment of the specific situation they face, and then they try to adapt their classroom environment accordingly.

You can do it too. Begin by exploring variability in societal values with your pupils. Such a frank study will prepare your pupils for the complexities of adult life. But better yet, it should diminish a good many behavior problems you'll face this year.

Adapt the suggestions in this chapter to your grade level and curricular expectations. Two approaches present themselves: (1) incorporate the material into language arts, health, and social studies units you normally teach during the year, or (2) develop the material into an occasional series of informal units that specifically study the school in our society.

DISCOVER VALUE VARIABILITY IN NEWSPAPERS

The local newspaper is an excellent place to begin your exploration of the variation that exists in the values held in your community. Ask your pupils to bring yesterday's paper to school, or the newspaper itself might be willing to provide copies for everyone. Develop your study of variation in community values around the edition of the paper you select.

The layout of a newspaper is interesting in itself. Note the somewhat disjointed way in which local and world stories of joy and tragedy are set side by side. A newspaper doesn't tell a single continuous story as a novel does, but rather it presents a mélange of events placed on the page like a jigsaw puzzle. Why not? The day was actually composed of random disjointed events. The newspaper reader doesn't have to read the entire paper to get the essence of what happened during the day. He can sample the paper, just as he sampled the events that were occurring around him all day long.

Begin your study at this point. The editors made initial value decisions that determined which news events would be included in their journal of the day's activities, and which would be excluded. They made these decisions partly on the basis of their beliefs about what is newsworthy. Proud parents might want their first-born's arrival heralded on page 1, and distraught parents certainly hope their son's arrest for bank robbery will be kept out of the paper. Chances are, both sets of parents will be disappointed.

Once editors select stories for inclusion, they use layout, headlines, and pictures to attract the reader to those stories they consider most significant. Editors also influence readers through the use of emotion laden headline terms such as thug, socialite, juvenile delinquent, rioters, concerned parents, and the like. See what your pupils can tell you about the editors' and publisher's values, or their view of the world that day by examining the layout of the newspaper.

Next, look closely at the news stories to discover the amount and variety of good news and bad news reported. Note also news items that imply community disagreement on values. Stories dealing with political, business, and labor issues are often of this type. If your pupils tabulate the column inches of news items devoted to these categories, they will probably discover that newspapers tend to report more bad news than good news, and more news on community disagreements than on agreement. Explore this phenomenon with your pupils. (One interesting theory is that newspapers balance all their bad news with advertisements, conceived of as good news for a better life.)

Several parts of the newspaper deal frankly with differences of opinion, and pupils should examine these carefully. Look at the editorial page first. The editorials, columnists, political cartoons, and letters to the editor all express interesting and conflicting points of view. If possible, find a single community or national issue that is discussed in several places on the page, and note the variety of opinions expressed. How does opinion writing differ from news reporting?

The special feature sections of the paper (sports section, women's page, amusement section, financial page, etc.) also describe differing values people hold. An article describing an important bowling tournament might be of absolutely no interest to a reader who is, however, excited about an announcement of a coming musical attraction. The various columns that give advice (beauty, lovelorn, senior citizens, parents, etc.) also provide excellent source material to use in your search for variability in values within your community—and in the nation since many of these columns are syndicated nationally. Such specialized features as crossword puzzles and astrological predictions also exist because of differing interests of readers.

If your community has several TV channels, examine last evening's programming as reported in the paper. How much choice did viewers have? Develop categories of interests (news, comedy, drama, discussion, sports, music, etc.) and determine which interests were taken care of during each half hour block, and how much choice viewers had throughout the evening.

Don't slight the comics. They're a special case of value communication. Children love the comics because the cartoonist writes only four or five brief segment's of the day's story, and thus he encourages the reader to imagine all the things that might happen between the boxes, and to mentally add details to the drawings. He involves his readers. Select a comic strip and ask your pupils to write what beliefs or values they think the cartoonist is trying to communicate with his comic strip. Your pupils might be surprised to discover how much their answers differ. The reason is, of course, that each person interprets the comic strip in the way he wishes to interpret it, because he brings his own set of values into his involvement with the developing story.

The advertisements in a newspaper also communicate much about a community's values. Advertisers spend large sums of money and take great pains to communicate their beliefs in their products. Note how they often try to identify their products with their customers' values—cleanliness, good times, romance, happiness, economy, sophistication, comfort, etc. Select one of these values and ask your pupils to see how often it is used or implied in the advertisements placed in the newspaper. Note also the classified ads. What things are put up for private sale? Why? What values are implied? Ask your pupils to select a classified ad in which household items are put up for sale, and to create a story that would explain the reason for the sale.

Using the newspaper to discover the existence of differences in values will lead you and your class to the next aspect of your investigation into conflicting societal values: the procedures people use to communicate what they do value.

Each person's experiences, beliefs, and values are bound up within his body—hidden from view. Our inner self meets the outside world where the outer layers of skin touch the air, and it is at this point that we communicate whatever we communicate about ourselves.

We have three principal means of communicating our values—our skin, our language, and our actions. Your pupils will enjoy exploring these, and they will learn much about themselves and the world about them in the process. Begin with the most intriguing of the three, skin.

COMMUNICATE VALUES THROUGH SKIN

The outer layers of our skin, our hair, and our nails are all dead, and yet we spend an inordinate amount of time and energy trying to make them look alive. There appears to be a bit of the mortician in most of us.

In our zeal, we've founded entire industries to assist us in this compulsion to adorn our dead skin. Cosmetics add a bit of color. Wave sets and rollers curl the hair. All sorts of false things are added where the wearer's own collection of hair, nails, and skin is deemed insufficient. Heat lamps turn light skin to the proper shade of tan (a sort of earth color that seems fitting). Sweet smelling lotions, perfumes, and deodorants add a macabre touch—and all to no avail.

Our hair, nails, and outer layers of skin are dead. Nothing can be done to bring them back to life. Look further down if you seek life.

Not that skin isn't important. We'd be in trouble without it. It keeps body heat in, infection out, and our insides in place. Although we do some rather bizarre things with our skin's surface, there is really an important side to skin adornment. We communicate much about ourselves and our values through these top layers of our skin, even though they are dead. It's a strange commentary on our society and its values, though, that we condone and even encourage so much deceit in what we thus communicate about ourselves.

Begin your study of communicating values through the skin with a brief examination of the structure and nature of the skin. Among other things your pupils will discover that it is the largest organ in the body. It weighs about six pounds and covers about twenty square feet spread out. Since it covers everything that comes in contact with the outside world, skin is also found inside the body in such places as the mouth, nose, lungs and intestinal tract.

You can discover many things about a person by looking at his skin and hair, and a number of these relate to values. Your pupils will probably suggest that they can often guess a person's approximate age by looking at his skin and hair. People who do outdoor and manual work often show it through their skin. Other things generally communicated through skin and hair are race, sex, state of health, and views on cleanliness and neatness.

Move rapidly from your brief examination of the structure and function of the skin to the more important study of the social significance of the skin and its extensions. By the time pupils reach the intermediate grades they are already emotionally involved in such societal conflicts as where and when and how much skin should be covered and uncovered, and where and when it should be adorned with cosmetics.

Clothes are the principal extension of our skin. They have a utilitarian value far beyond anything modesty might require. We'd have to eat much more food if we didn't wear clothes, because of the heat loss. Thus, clothing, as an extension of skin, helps us store and channel body energy.

Clothes also give us far more flexibility than skin in adornment. We are able to drape and color this second layer of skin in an unlimited variety of ways. Consequently, clothes permit us to communicate more subtle values, and values more subtly. Develop this idea with your class by writing a list of words such as these on the board: mink, bridal gown, diapers, jersey, overalls, nylon, miniskirt, pink, scarf, heels, uniforms. Each of these terms is loaded with social and style implications and sanctions that can be brought out in a class discussion. Little girls usually don't wear mink and big boys usually don't wear pink. Pupils will probably respond in such conventional ways initially, but the discussion should lead to ways in which these conventions are disregarded when styles change. Today is certainly such a time of great flux in clothing styles.

Your pupils might want to try to effect a style change in your school, perhaps by wearing a common article of clothing differently, or by adding a simple ornamentation (remember pennies in loafers?) that others could adopt easily. They will learn much about the dynamics of style change by observing their own success or failure in establishing a style, and by discussing such questions as: Why do people follow a new style? What does a style change communicate? Why do parents often dislike the new styles of young people? Are there any limits to possible style changes? What roles does the fashion industry play in establishing fashions? What advantages accrue to stores and manufacturers when styles change?

One interesting aspect of clothing that's fun to explore is the purely ornamental article of clothing—jewelry, cuffs, extra buttons, lapels, lace, and the like. Ask pupils to examine their clothes to see how many such items they can find. Why do people add this ornamentation to their clothes? Why are these ornaments frequently quite expensive? Why are some ornaments (rings, pins) used to communicate specific things about the wearer such as marital status or membership in organizations? Why do some people enjoy wearing jewelry while others never wear it? Your pupils' answers to questions such as these will be speculative, but the discussions should help them look more closely at clothes as agents that communicate what we believe and our values.

Encourage your pupils to bring pictures of current clothing styles to school ·Discuss these in terms of what the clothing tells about the wearer. Note how utility and ornament are combined. Does form follow function? How does mass production tend to eliminate social class distinctions in the clothes we wear? How does the environment affect the clothes we wear? Why would we feel strange in a swimming suit at school, or in school clothes at the beach? Do men dress more sensibly than women, or vice versa? Why do schools often make regulations about the clothes and hair styles pupils wear, and why are these regulations often different for boys and girls? Why do parents differ in what they will permit their children to wear? Why do some schools ask pupils to wear uniforms?

It's difficult to say where all these questions will take you and your class, but it will certainly be interesting to find out. Once you accept the premise that skin serves a useful purpose in that it helps regulate our body's temperature, and that it communicates certain things about ourselves—and that clothing serves these same functions—then you're only a hop and skip away from some wilder ideas.

Ready? Is a house a third layer of skin? Does it keep heat in? Does it keep our family and belongings in place? Does it also serve as a form of adornment that communicates things about us to people who pass by? If a house is a third layer of skin, then when we put on an overcoat upon leaving the house, do we take off the house and put on the overcoat?

More? Are air conditioners and furnaces a layer of skin, once removed? What is the relationship between man and animals in the matter of dress? Why do people wear uniforms? What is the social significance of attractive underwear? What kind of clothes should a non-conformist wear? What about medieval walled cities? Is a car a layer of skin en route?

We tend to take skin and clothes for granted, but they do communicate much to others about what we are and what we believe. Thus, they can serve as an excellent and intriguing introduction to the study of varying and conflicting social values.

COMMUNICATE VALUES THROUGH LANGUAGE

Although our skin and clothes communicate much about what we are and believe, language provides a much broader and deeper base for communication. Skin and clothes are surface communicators. Language comes from within.

One of the problems with skin and clothes is that their instant communicative nature often encourages us to classify people too rapidly. Language usually takes longer. If we can talk with a person over a period of time, we can generally develop a more accurate picture of him and his values. Thus, while a man's shabby clothes and unshaven face might communicate Skid Row at first glance, his conversation might communicate a far different picture—perhaps even that he's a wealthy man just back from a hunting trip. Language permits us to expand on what we are and believe with a clarity that skin and clothes can rarely match.

Chapter One suggested ways in which you could introduce your pupils to the basic nature of communication through language. Continue this investigation with your pupils, concentrating now on the problems man faces when he attempts to communicate his beliefs and values through words.

Your pupils will soon discover that while language is a magnificent communication tool, it is not foolproof. Words can never describe values completely, and this often leads to unhappiness in social relations. A family argument develops because a comment was misunderstood. A pupil breaks into tears because he took his teacher's criticism the wrong way. A child has difficulty trying to explain the exact nature of the sick feeling that encompasses him.

Use word games to introduce your pupils to the shifting meaning of words. For example, ask your pupils to develop pairs of statements that use (almost) the same words, but that communicate different meanings. "Did she keep the clean house for herself?" "Did she clean the house for her keep?"—"Now, don't be long!" "I don't belong now." Homonyms help sometimes. "The boy understood the girl." "The girl stood under the buoy."

"Gossip" is a common game in which an adjective and adverb loaded sentence is whispered from person to person around a circle. (For example: The wild-eyed bear viciously attacked the three sweet babies while their mothers picked berries nearby.) The players then compare the sentence heard by the last person in the circle with the sentence said by the first person. It's usually quite different. Use a tape recorder to play a variation on this game. Arrange things so that pupils can whisper into a microphone and the next person's ear at the same time. Replay the entire tape after the statement has been passed on to everyone, and your class will be able to note when and how changes were made in the original sentence. Use this experience to lead your class into a discussion of the difficulties man encounters when he relies on oral language—the ears and speech of several people—to pass information to a destination.

Another interesting variation on this game uses pictures instead of words. Make a simple line drawing with few details, perhaps only a house and a tree. Give each pupil in your class a sheet of the same kind of paper you used. Show your drawing to one pupil for ten seconds, and ask him to reproduce it on his paper. Then show *his* drawing to the next pupil for ten seconds and ask that pupil to reproduce what he saw. Continue in this fashion through the entire class. Display all the drawings in sequence, noting where adaptations occurred. You and your pupils will be amazed at the variety of changes—and your pupils will profit from a slightly different look at some of the complexities of communication.

"Rhopalons" illustrates changes a word can go through when single letters are added. Pupils enjoy "rhopalons," and at the same time they gain a deeper appreciation for the subtle shifts in meaning that exist in language. Begin with a one or two letter word and add letters one at a time, forming a new word with each additional letter. For example: O, on, ton, torn, thorn, hornet, thrones, shortens.

Demonstrate the tremendous variety that exists in our language by introducing your class to Roget's *Thesaurus*. Select a common adjective and ask one or two pupils to use the thesaurus to develop a list of all possible synonyms for that word. Discuss their list and the various shades of meaning that exist in our language for the idea or the value expressed through that adjective.

Song is one of the most interesting weddings of word and value. The singer uses lyrics to tell his story, and melody to create the mood that adds depth and feeling to the lyrics. Find examples of songs with melodies that definitely communicate an emotion (joy, humor, excitement, etc.). First play the melody to see if the pupils can guess the mood. Then read the lyrics to see if your pupils are correct. On the next song reverse the process. Note how both words and music are often needed to tell the story in its mood context in such songs as Brahm's Lullaby, "Jingle Bells," and "The Caissons Go Rolling Along."

Ask two pupils to prepare oral presentations that inform the class of something pleasant coming up later in the day. One pupil should merely give his classmates a straight factual presentation. The other pupil should become excited about the coming activity and express his feelings as strongly as possible while he presents the necessary information. Compare the two presentations with your class to determine what the second pupil did to the basic information to convey his feelings on the subject.

It's interesting to compare written and spoken language. One way to do this is to do or say something to your class that would normally elicit an oral response such as ugh, ouch, wow, or a laugh. Note how one short word or sound suffices when the reaction is oral. Then ask your pupils to convey the same reaction in writing, without using the oral expression they used earlier. They may need to use quite a few words because oral communication can use speech inflections that are difficult to convey in writing. This is especially true of expletives.

These language activities and discussions should help your pupils discover that the world is filled with people who hold many different values and beliefs. All these people must use words to communicate their values to others, hoping that the others will understand and accept them—or at least tolerate them.

Your classroom is a microcosm of society, so you and your pupils should welcome such variability in values and the opportunity to work together to discover more effective ways for people of similar and different backgrounds and beliefs to communicate verbally with each other.

COMMUNICATE VALUES THROUGH ACTIONS

A surprisingly large number of common expressions deal with man's attempts to communicate his values through actions. For example: "Actions speak louder than words." "Sticks and stones may break my bones but words can never fell me." "Suit the action to the word, the word to the action." "To live is not merely to breathe, it is to act." "Execute every act of your life as though it were your last."

While some of these expressions have become trite in the adult world, your pupils probably haven't explored their meaning yet—and they should. It's really quite exciting for a child to discover the close relationships that exist between a person's values and his behavior. We're so close to our own actions and to the actions of others that we don't often see what is right in front of us.

You'll probably get the best response from your pupils if you begin your class study by examining the many values we can communicate through simple physical contact. Work together to develop a list of words that describe forms of physical contact. Your pupils will be amazed at the large number of such words that exist—hit, caress, spank, embrace, punch, kick, pet, scratch, slap, kiss, shake hands, and wrestle, to name just a few. Arrange the words on a chart placing them in categories that show what values the actions express (such as love, friendship, fear, anger, etc.). Discuss the different shades of meaning we communicate through the actions placed in each category (for example: pinch, nip, squeeze, etc.). Note how some of the words can be included in several categories depending on the intensity of the action.

Ask your pupils to keep track of all physical contacts made during a school day, and then tabulate these on the chart described above. Can your class conclude anything about the nature of the relationships that exist in the class by examining this tabulation? Did pupils vary in the kinds of physical contacts they experienced? What differences exist between boys' and girls' reports?

Many games are based on physical contact or avoidance of contact: football, basketball, hockey, boxing, wrestling, soccer, etc. Some non-contact games (such as volleyball and tennis) actually use a net to separate the competing players. All these games are based on values that stress competition. Players work singly or in teams to demonstrate their athletic superiority. They wear distinctive uniforms, and they give themselves names such as Bears, Lions, Rockets, and Giants to proclaim their superiority.

Explore the sports phenomenon with your pupils by discussing such ideas as these: Football is a game of contact, and yet the runners who can escape contact with the opposing team are the most highly regarded (halfbacks, ends, etc.). The object of many games (basketball, soccer, etc.) is to avoid physical contact with the opposing team in order to gain and maintain possession of a ball both teams covet. Many games use referees to determine if physical contact between opposing players is proper. Thousands of people will crowd into a stadium to watch two football teams charge into each other, but each of these spectators wants a separate space in the stands, and he tries to enter and leave the stadium with a minimum of crowd jostling. More men than women appear to enjoy the major spectator sports in our country.

Discuss the values sports enthusiasts claim for sports. Can your pupils see parallels in normal life? Is that why our society has such a tremendous interest in sports? What purpose do sports rules and rituals serve? Why do people like to watch contact sports when relatively few of them would actually want to participate in the game itself?

Move from sports to an examination of the behavior of people under crowded conditions. The more crowded people are, the more effort they make to avoid having direct contact with each other. Thus, people crowded together in a large city apartment building will normally make few efforts to get acquainted with neighbors a thin wall away, while isolated ranchers try to maintain contact with neighbors miles away. Watch large groups of people together in a crowded space such as a corridor, on a sidewalk or playground, or in a department store in December. Note what steps people take to avoid physical contact with each other. A touch brings an apology, and that's generally the only verbal contact they have too. We live lonely in a crowd.

As a society we seem to value our touch. It isn't something to be passed around indiscriminately. We touch those we like or dislike, but not those with whom we have no emotional attachment.

This suggests that your pupils might be able to examine the dimensions of physical contact in their classroom. It shouldn't take them long to note that much of the misbehavior that occurs in a classroom is related to unwanted physical contact—jostling, fighting, shoving. If they can see the similarities between the problems physical contact causes in life and in their classroom, they will develop a better understanding of behavior problems that affect the smooth operation of their class group.

While we have concentrated our attention on actions involving physical contact, we do communicate values through other actions also, and you should explore these with your pupils too. For example, the gesture, smile, wave, frown, tears, and wink all communicate expressions of value. Explore also the action that communicates love or acceptance through a helping hand, through a gift—or that communicates rejection through an act of vandalism, through a theft. Relate these and the values they support to classroom life.

Through these explorations, your pupils will develop an understanding of the many ways in which man communicates his values and beliefs in the things that he does.

EXAMINE VALUES THROUGH MONEY

"Put your money where your mouth is" is a common expression that demonstrates the significance of money in our society's value system. Any school investigation into the nature of value and value conflict in our society can profit much by examining the nature of money. Eventually most of our value decisions relate to money in some way. We buy what we want and can afford. We sell what we don't need. We live where we work. We bank money for a rainy day. We borrow money to take a vacation trip.

In a simple society, each person takes care of his own needs and wants. His actions are direct and are related to the specific task at hand—to get food, to build shelter, to relax.

As a society becomes more complex, a division of labor takes place. It becomes difficult for each person to take care of all his own needs directly. He lacks the skills, materials, facilities, and time. Commodity and service trading is a natural consequence. I have more meat than I can eat before it spoils. You have more bricks than you need to provide for your shelter, and I need bricks. Let's trade.

The next step is to trade in future acquisitions. I would like to have some of your bricks, but I have no meat now. Give me your bricks today and I'll give you meat the next time I hunt. In a simple society, a person's promise is sufficient.

It's not sufficient, or even efficient, in a complex society. We've so fragmented our needs and efforts, and we've involved such a large group of people in even the simplest transactions, that we need a system of exchange that can reduce everything to a common standard that can cover the entire realm of social interaction. Thus, commodity exchange becomes currency exchange, and gold has become our common standard of exchange. Money, then, is a promise on both sides of the barter to exchange a commodity or service for another commodity or service without expending the necessary energy at the time of the transaction. So whenever money is received and held, it becomes frozen energy—ready for thawing and use whenever our sense of value determines that another exchange should take place.

Since this process relates so directly to our value system, it is a fascinating and important process to explore with your pupils. One of the best ways to do it is through games. Many popular children's games (e.g. Monopoly) revolve around money. Play games with currency that is based on something other than our gold standard, though, since this will focus attention on the idea of currency and value instead of on the currency itself. The thought of playing the following game in school may terrify you, but you don't really have to play it to grasp its economic and value subtleties. Present the rules to your class, and then just discuss what would happen if you played the game, and how these occurrences would relate to a monetary system and to a system of values. Of course, if you don't mind a little mess and confusion, try playing it or your own variation on it.

Use ice cubes and balloons for money. Give each child one large balloon, two small ones, and ten ice cubes. The value of this money is determined by their weight rather than their state, so you'll need some small scales.

Ask pupils to buy and sell real or make believe commodities and services during the school day. They could sharpen pencils for each other, run errands, or sell candy and gum. They can rent space in thermos jugs, create insurance companies, or combine their wealth in corporations. In every transaction, though, pupils will make decisions based on their set of values.

Since the ice cubes (frozen money) will mélt, they will decrease in value during the day unless some way can be found to maintain their weight even though they melt. It won't be long before pupils will think of placing their ice cubes inside the balloons so they won't lose their weight when they turn to water. Balloons will then increase in value since they can be used to maintain the shrinking weight and value of the melting ice cubes. Another advantage is that water can be divided into smaller weight units more easily than ice cubes.

Problems will arise and counterfeiting will be one of these. Some pupils might fill their balloons with tap water, or bring additional ice cubes and balloons from home at noon. Such problems should lead to a discussion of the need for currency that can't be counterfeited, and the possible effects of counterfeiting on the stability of money. It could also lead to discussions on inflation, on the shifting value of money, and on the nature and need for honesty in a complex society.

Conspicuous consumption is another problem that relates directly to differing values. Some pupils may discover that it's more fun to eat or to destroy their ice cubes than to trade them. Others will be aghast at such extravagance and will complain that such pupils "aren't playing fair." This situation also creates possibilities for discussions on relative values in our society. How much money should be spent on a wedding, on clothes, on a vacation? What does it mean to waste money? Why save money? Is gambling wrong? Is it wrong to deliberately destroy food or money? Is there a difference between the two?

The most interesting discovery will be made at the end

of the day when pupils weigh their balloons full of water to determine who is the richest person in the room. That's the time to ask the winner what he has really achieved for all his efforts. The answer to this question should provide the basis for fascinating discussions in the days ahead as you probe the ways in which this game provided a correct and incorrect model of a monetary system, and as you move from the mechanics of economics of the values that underlie any such system.

And the questions you can raise! Is a motion picture a success if it makes money and a failure if it doesn't? How much is a painting worth? Does a man's worth increase dramatically if oil is discovered on his land? Should governments support space research and welfare programs? Should a businessman use business profits to contribute to charity without asking his customers (who provided the profits) which charities to support? What good does it do to have a lot of money when rich and poor alike can watch the same TV shows and movies and breathe the same air? How many pairs of shoes does a person need?

Use these discussions to lead your class to the value conflicts and frustrations people always face in a social setting. For example, an employer determines when his employees must report for work, and this decision is not generally made on the basis of how far away a given employee might live, or what time he got to bed last night—but rather on the needs of the company. Each person who works for a company usually has his own ideas on how things ought to be done, but the employer and all his employees must finally agree to patterns of behavior that all accept. In any social organization the individual must adapt his values and wishes to the needs of the entire group and to the institution itself if the institution is to accomplish its task.

This is never easy. As individuals, we don't want to lose our identity, and we fear we will if we always give in to the desires of others. It is precisely this concern that leads to much of what we call classroom misbehavior. The pupil whose value system is similar to the school's preferred values has less difficulty adjusting to school than the pupil with a radically different set of values. The latter will either become very frustrated in school, or else he will fight all attempts to change his values and beliefs.

While the activities suggested in this chapter will not solve all your classroom behavior problems, they will encourage the sort of frank teacher-pupil discussion that helps children understand why they feel the way they do, and act the way they do.

It's always difficult to find individuality in a social situation. The kinds of exploration described in this chapter are the first steps a class should take to resolve the frustrations they will face during a year of working together.

THREE

Projecting Responsible Adult

Society in Your Classroom

The variety of values society accepts and the nature of classroom instruction places teachers in a position where they can promote a wide assortment of values. It's probably true that you could promote almost any set of values in your classroom and find that some people in your community would accept them without question.

Promoting values and promoting values successfully are two different things, however. You will be successful in transferring your values and beliefs to pupils only if you are the kind of person your pupils would accept as a model. You should be permitted to promote your values in elementary classrooms only if you promote a responsible set of values. And you will be permitted to promote your values in a given elementary school only if your values fall within the broadly or narrowly defined limits that community establishes—as defined by school officials.

But that's the problem. What is a good model? What is a responsible set of values? What values dominate in your community? In short, how can you make best use of the 1000 hours society gives you to place your values on display before a classroom full of children?

Chapter Two suggested ways in which you and your pupils could examine the variability in values that exists in society. This chapter will suggest ways in which you can narrow that examination to yourself and to the values you represent. Your pupils will profit from the examination, and so will you. Classroom relationships and behavior are generally best where pupils and teachers understand the roles both fulfill.

KNOW WHAT SOCIETY EXPECTS OF YOU

Most people have opinions on teachers and teaching. No other profession reaches as many people over such a long period of time as does teaching. And while most people hesitate to second-guess surgeons, they are willing—and frequently eager—to second-guess teachers and teaching. Note how many letters on the editorial page of your local paper refer to school issues.

There's nothing wrong with listening to or even seeking out such lay advice as long as you do it professionally—with an open mind. When you meet people, don't hesitate to introduce yourself as an elementary teacher, identifying your school and grade. Inevitably, they will comment on teachers and teaching. Listen carefully. It isn't necessary to agree with these people, and it isn't necessary to argue with them. But it is important that you listen respectfully, and that you do what you can to clarify misunderstandings or to rectify mistakes. It's far better that patrons feel free to express their concerns and views to school people at any time, rather than wait until they can lump everything together into negative votes on school issues.

It's also important that you hear such sentiments from a broad spectrum of the community. Seek ways to broaden your interests and contacts in the community. Don't associate only with other teachers. Seek out clubs and organizations to which few teachers belong, that aren't related to school life. You will gain a perspective from these contacts that will give you a better idea of what your community expects from you.

Schools of today have a responsibility that extends far beyond the confines of any school district, however. Our society is so mobile that it's necessary to be concerned about the values and opinions of many other groups of people.

The mass media have done much to create a national awareness of differing values. This suggests that you should read newspapers and magazines, go to the movies, watch TV, listen to current songs, attend lectures, and read books. Seriously consider subscribing to magazines with editorial policies you don't accept, and watching TV programs and movies you don't particularly enjoy as you go about discovering our society and its values.

You might not like everything you see and hear, but what you see and hear are aspects of our culture, and you should know and try to understand more of our culture than the typical individual in our society understands. After all, you are a professional interpreter of our culture, and you're going to have to interpret it at a very elementary level at that. Be curious. Seek variety. Keep your eyes and ears open to cultural changes that will affect your pupils' lives. You're going to have to filter the essence of our culture through your own personality so that your pupils see it as a function of a real live person, and not as an abstraction. For example, the term *fashion* means little to elementary school children, but they do know how you dress, and how your clothes compare with what others wear. Or, the idea of memorizing poetry might not appeal to intermediate grade pupils at all, but they do know the lyrics of many of the popular songs and they delight in singing them.

WATCH OUT FOR PROBLEM AREAS

Most people are sympathetic with the complexity of your role as a teacher, and so they are willing to grant a wide zone of tolerance in the values you espouse. You can tell your pupils that you love asparagus and dislike turnips, that you enjoy golf but see little sense in hunting, that you appreciate Mozart but find Bach stuffy—and you can rest assured that your patrons will not march on the school board to protest.

There are several areas, however, where your patrons will not always be so willing to grant you license to say what you will to your pupils. Chief among these are the values you hold with respect to religion, politics, patriotism, and propriety. Let's examine each of these areas a bit more closely.

Religion

Before I began public school teaching, I was a bit concerned about what I would say if pupils asked about my religious beliefs and practices. My first confrontation happened sooner than I expected, and before I had prepared an answer. One fall day two of my sixth graders asked me if I went to church. Without thinking or even hesitating, I replied that I attended the Lutheran Church—and then I asked them if they attended church. One told me he attended the Methodist Church, and the other said he and his dad liked to hunt and fish on weekends. To each response I said something like, "Well, that's nice," and that was that.

The issue had come up, and I had responded to it—sensibly, I would argue. My pupils had asked a proper question, and they deserved a forthright answer. They didn't ask to be indoctrinated. They just asked for information. In retrospect, I don't know today why I was so concerned about what I would say in answer to that question.

As teachers, we have to differentiate between informing our pupils about religion and indoctrinating them in a religion. The former can be a very proper function of the public school. The church has always been a vibrant part of our national heritage, and it is ridiculous to suggest, by ignoring it, that the church doesn't exist. It is perfectly proper for you to belong to any church or to no church, and it is equally proper to tell your pupils whether or not you belong to a church if the sub-ject comes up—and if you wish to tell them. You should also feel free to answer other legitimate questions your pupils might ask about the beliefs and practices of your church or of other churches—and so you might want to occasionally attend various churches in your community so you'll know a bit more about them.

Unfortunately, a free and easy classroom exchange of in-formation about churches can easily lead into discussions and comments that border on missionary efforts. This is not a proper function of the public school. Watch yourself, so that you don't get carried away by what you say and how you say it. As a teacher you have a forum that permits you to display your views in their most favorable light. If you emphasize your denominational preference throughout the school year, you are, in effect, promoting a church instead of the values it espouses. Let your religious convictions shine through your dealings with others. The denominational tag is much less important in your classroom than the way in which you live your beliefs.

Most parents would probably agree that it's good for chil-dren to come into contact with adults of various religious per-suasions during their school years, but it's also probably safe to say that many of these same parents would hope that teachers whose religious beliefs are radically different from theirs won't be too persuasive when they promote their beliefs. And that's the rub.

Be what you are. That's all you can be. If you are a very religious person your pupils will have the experience of work-ing with a very religious teacher. If organized religion means nothing to you, your pupils will work with a teacher who draws values from sources other than the established religions. What-ever your persuasion, it's good for your pupils to know the source of your behavior—but it's not proper for you to engage in activities that smack of proselytizing or cause dissension. The distinction is a fine one, but it's one that public school teach-ers must conscientiously establish and maintain.

Politics

Politics and religion are similar in some ways. Both make a strong appeal to the emotions through forms, rituals, and symbols. Both deal with man's attempts to reach an ideal state through behavior that usually falls short of perfection. Every church and every political party is made up of a membership with (often widely) differing opinions about what the organization should do. Interest and activity tends to fluctuate, increasing greatly at certain times (such as religious festivals and elections) and diminishing somewhat at other times. Finally, it's often difficult for elementary pupils to understand the distinctions that separate the various churches or the various political parties.

By and large, people are more apt to be closely associated with an organized church than with a political party organization. It also seems that they are also generally less concerned about an elementary teacher's political views than about his religious views—unless his views are quite extreme.

As an elementary teacher, you should have and demonstrate a sincere interest in politics. You should vote in every election, and theoretically you should feel free to discuss coming elections with your pupils. There is nothing intrinsically wrong with telling your pupils how you plan to vote, if you want to tell them. Your pupils should begin to realize that some people don't like to tell others how they vote—and that's what the secret ballot is all about; but that others like to express their political views—and that's what political parties are all about. It would be nice if the issue was always as simple as this, but it often isn't. Emotions can and do run high in some elections, and teachers have to respond with common sense at such times, limiting their discussion of the election to contacts with other adults.

If you tell your pupils how you plan to vote in an election you will, of course, express opinions that differ from the opinions of other adults. You should then also try to present the other side of the issue as objectively as you can, and hopefully your pupils will also hear it presented by other teachers, their parents, and through the mass media. Be concerned that your pupils get a balanced account of the arguments on both sides of the issue, and be willing to admit that your presentation of both sides is a biased presentation.

Try to bring in someone who holds an opposing view to yours so that your pupils can hear how two responsible adults thought through the same issue and came to different conclusions. Children need to know that a democratic society will always contain citizens with contrasting views on any issue under discussion, and that responsible adults think through the issues before arriving at their own conclusions.

Consider the alternatives. In a democratic society every issue has its proponents, its opponents, and the apathetic. The apathetic tend to be a consistent group, apathetic about almost every political issue. It's not a good group to draw teachers from. It's better that we staff our schools with teachers who have opinions, who vigorously confront the issues of the day, whatever their convictions, even though school problems might arise from it—than it is to have teachers who rarely confront a political issue or express a political view in 1000 hours of close contact with pupils.

We need to be less concerned about partisan teachers and more concerned about apathetic teachers. The former tend to balance out over the years, and their pupils learn from them to judge when reason gives way to pure emotionalism. The latter do little but encourage another generation to become apathetic adults. And who wants that?

Patriotism

Ask the next ten people you see if they can repeat the second, third or fourth stanzas of our National Anthem. Chances are that not more than one or two can—if that many.

To some people patriotism means the National Anthem, the flag, and the Fourth of July. To others it means paying your taxes cheerfully. To others it means being willing to criticize your country when you feel it should be criticized. To still others it can mean other and more personal things. And each person is convinced that his definition of patriotism is the best one.

The typical elementary pupil isn't really aware of his country—its heritage, its greatness, its potential, its problems. A patriotic teacher can do much to help develop that awareness.

It's important to differentiate between chauvinism and patriotism. The former is superpatriotism, a blind and boastful devotion to our country that does little credit to the zealot or to his country, and that presents a distorted picture of our country that elementary schools shouldn't present. In essence, it suggests that every decision our country has made was correct, and that everything about our country is just about perfect.

On the other hand, elementary teachers shouldn't constantly emphasize the opposite point of view either—a negativism that finds failure in practically everything our country has done, that sees only the problems that remain to be solved, and ignores the real advances that have been made in solving them.

Somewhere between these two extreme positions is the position you should take as an elementary teacher. During the year your pupils are with you they should get to know a teacher who honestly loves his country and all its emotional forms, rituals, and problems. But they should also get to know a teacher who sees much more in his country than wars and famous men and inventions. The essence of our country's strength has always been its genius for using democratic procedures to solve complex problems in a complex society. And because we try to solve our problems democratically, it generally takes us a long time to solve them, if we solve them at all. The elementary school introduces children to the joys, the frustrations, and the complexities of democratic action. Thus, it prepares them to be responsible and patriotic citizens.

Thus the properly patriotic elementary teacher can easily become emotional whenever he sees the flag—and whenever he sees prejudice. He can become very helpful whenever he's asked to contribute to a worthy cause—and whenever he sees litter on the sidewalk. He conscientiously and honestly makes out his income tax return. And he has at least *read* the second, third, and fourth stanzas of "The Star Spangled Banner."

1. O say, can you see, by the dawn's early light,
    What so proudly we hail'd at the twilight's last gleaming?
   Whose broad stripes and bright stars, thro' the perilous fight,
    O'er the ramparts we watch'd, were so galantly streaming?
   And the rockets' red glare, the bombs bursting in air,
    Gave proof thro' the night that our flag was still there.
    O say, does that star-spangled banner yet wave
    O'er the land of the free and the home of the brave?

2. On the shore dimly seen thro' the mists of the deep,
    Where the foe's haughty host in dread silence reposes,
   What is that which the breeze, o'er the towering steep,
    As it fitfully blows, half conceals, half discloses?
   Now it catches the gleam of the morning's first beam,
    In full glory reflected now shines on the stream:
    'Tis the star-spangled banner: oh long may it wave
    O'er the land of the free and the home of the brave!

3. And where is that band who so vauntingly swore
    Mid the havoc of war and the battle's confusion
   A home and a country should leave us no more?
    Their blood has washed out their foul footsteps' pollution.
   No refuge could save the hireling and slave
    From the terror of flight or the gloom of the grave:
    And the star-spangled banner in triumph doth wave
    O'er the land of the free and the home of the brave.

4. Oh, thus be it ever when freemen shall stand
    Between their loved home and the wild war's desolation;
   Blest with victory and peace, may the heav'n-rescued land
    Praise the pow'r that hath made and preserved us a nation!
   Then conquer we must, when our cause it is just,
    And this be our motto: "In God is our trust!"
    And the star-spangled banner in triumph shall wave
    O'er the land of the free and the home of the brave.

Propriety

Should an elementary teacher work in a bar on weekends to supplement teaching income? Probably not. What's wrong with working in a bar? Nothing. Bars are a perfectly legitimate business so it should be proper for any adult to work in one. And yet, many experienced educators would advise elementary teachers against working in a bar as a moonlighting vocation— particularly in a small community. It's just one aspect of a hard-to-pin-down and frequently frustrating issue called propriety.

Happily, we've come a long way since the days when a woman teacher would lose her job if she married, when teachers were expected to be faithful in their church attendance, when it was unheard of for a teacher to smoke in public.

Even so the specter of propriety still haunts the private life of elementary teachers. Elementary teachers can't escape the fact that they teach as much by what they are as they do by working with what is in the textbooks. A college teacher meets his students for perhaps three hours a week. The elementary teacher lives with his for thirty hours. Thus, an elementary teacher's private life merges with his public professional life, particularly in smaller communities, to the point where the propriety of any behavior must always be a live concern.

And the questions it raises: Is smoking advisable? Is it all right to wager on the World Series? What kind of clothes should I wear at school and while moving about the community? Is it wrong to frequent bars? Is it all right to use a lot of slang in conversations with pupils? What about cosmetics and hairdos? Must I attend church? May I attend any movie shown in community theaters? Should I even be concerned about the propriety of any situation just because I am a teacher?

How you answer questions such as these will depend somewhat on your personality and on the size and nature of the community you teach in, its expectations, and the amount of privacy it offers you during out-of-school hours. Three general guidelines might be helpful, though, in helping you decide on the propriety of a given action or practice:

1. Does the action or practice draw excessive attention to some part of your body or personality that you don't particularly want to emphasize?
2. Does the action or practice encourage behavior you wouldn't

want to encourage your pupils to participate in, either as children or later as adults?

3. Does the action or practice offend a substantial number of people who will speak disparagingly of teachers because of it?

The four problem areas discussed in this section provide you with opportunities to examine and confront yourself and your values under somewhat dramatic circumstances. You will probably profit as much, though, from an examination of your responses to the more routine aspects of your total school life. Let's turn to these next.

EXAMINE YOURSELF AND YOUR VALUES

Poets and philosophers have long lamented about how difficult it is for a person to develop an accurate picture of himself; and yet you owe it to yourself and to your pupils to make a serious effort to do just that. As a teacher you're always consciously or unconsciously communicating things about yourself to your pupils—and you should know what you're communicating.

In recent years various group techniques such as role playing and sensitivity training have helped many people develop a greater awareness of themselves. Explore these with your colleagues, since they do show some promise.

But you can also study yourself and your values privately in your own classroom. Begin with problems in which overt behavior of some sort brings your values to the surface, and then examine your responses. Three general areas lend themselves well to this kind of examination: the pressures of classroom life, classroom behavior annoyances, and interactions with other adults.

The Pressures of Classroom Life

Something is always going on in an elementary classroom, and usually it's a number of things at once. The typical elementary teacher makes hundreds of instructional and behavioral decisions every day with several pending at any given moment. Under these circumstances it's almost impossible for a teacher to put on any sort of consistent false front. You react instinctively—and thereby communicate much of your real self all day long. Examine these reactions carefully, and you can learn much about yourself.

Keep a brief informal record of classroom situations in which legitimate differences of opinion exist. Review your notes at the end of the day and ask yourself such questions as: What caused the problems? What opinions did I hold? Were the situations always resolved the way I wanted them resolved? Do certain kinds of problems arise in my classroom again and again? Are the same pupils generally involved? Which of my responses were proper, in retrospect, and which could be questioned? How might I handle similar situations differently in the future?

The tape recorder provides many opportunities to study yourself and your values. Tape segments of the school day from time to time: a lesson, the ten minutes before school begins, a class party, a study period, a class meeting. Replay these after school and listen carefully for comments that divulge things about yourself: for comments that give a different impression of yourself than the one you want to make, for comments that encourage and discourage, for humorous asides, for moralizing. You might also ask a colleague to listen with you and comment on the taped segment. Reciprocate by listening to and commenting on a taped segment of your colleague's day. Both of you will profit from the exchange of ideas.

The tape recorder can also be used profitably with the Flanders Interaction Analysis system. You can easily learn the system by studying the many materials developed on it, or by taking one of the short courses or workshops offered frequently about the country. What you do, essentially, is to tape a twenty minute lesson, replay it, and then categorize the classroom verbal interaction every three seconds. Placed into a matrix these judgments can reveal quite a bit about the kind of verbal interaction you establish in your classroom.

Create simple systems of your own, if you wish. For example, divide a sheet of ruled paper with a vertical line. Label the left side *positive* and the right side *negative*. Every fifteen minutes during the school day jot down your positive and negative reactions to the last fifteen minutes. After several days examine your comments to discover patterns of reactions. What kinds of things annoy you? What makes you happy? What kinds of things don't show up on either side? You might ask your pupils to keep the same kind of record for a day or so. Compare your responses with theirs. Do you find significant similarities and differences?

Classroom Annoyances

You can learn a lot about yourself by examining the classroom behavior that annoys you. Through the years quite a few research studies have investigated pupil behavior that annoys teachers. In general, the studies seem to indicate that teachers are most annoyed by overt actions of pupils that disrupt the smooth operation of the classroom, and that frustrate the teacher's authority. Many of these behaviors are normal for children, but teachers find them unpleasant—and some teachers consider them deliberate attempts to undermine their authority.

Jot down the specific behaviors that seem to annoy you the most. Can you group them into categories that tell you things about yourself and the way you teach? Do these behaviors occur frequently? How do you react when you are annoyed? Do you arrange activities so that such annoying behaviors are less apt to occur?

Ask your pupils to write down the things they think annoy you. You might be surprised to discover how much their lists agree with yours. They observe you carefully all day long. Do their lists show you to be the patient and tolerant person you think you are, or do you seem petty and worrisome to them? Are you more annoyed by boys' or by girls' behavior?

Where your examinations of your reactions to pupil behavior show that you communicate a different personality than the one you wish to communicate, seek other ways to respond to your pupils' behavior. (The later chapters in this book will offer specific suggestions.)

People You Work With

Elementary teaching is really quite a lonely occupation. Although you're working around people all the time, you make contact with other adults on surprisingly few occasions during the school day, and these are generally fleeting—a few moments in the faculty room, a brief conversation with another teacher while the two of you are supervising the playground, a relaxing half hour with a colleague after school, a conference with a parent, a bit of banter with the custodian.

Most of your contacts are with pupils; and since these contacts with the immature can place you under tension, you might reflect this tension in the contacts you do have with colleagues and other adults. Consider the petty interstaff arguments that often characterize life in an elementary school.

Try this to discover how you react to your colleagues and to adults who enter your school world. Withdraw from active participation during a coffee room discussion after school or during the lunch hour and merely react mentally to the comments and ideas that swirl about. Think about the nature of your reactions. Do you tend to side with certain members of the staff on most topics discussed and to reject the ideas of others? Do you find the discussion challenging or insipid? Do you prefer that such discussions revolve around professional issues or do you hope for a bit of respite from school talk when you get away from your pupils for a few minutes? It's probably true that your contemplations won't bring you to a point where you can identify right and wrong answers to such questions— assuming there are right and wrong answers—but you certainly should develop a better understanding of the feelings you have towards your colleagues just by being aware of your feelings.

Do you look forward to contacts with the parents of your pupils or do you dread them? If you dread them, ask yourself why. Is it because you are unsure of your relationships with your pupils? Is it because you fear the stories they might take home? Is it because you think parental expectations are greater than pupils can deliver? Relax. Parents are generally just as curious and anxious about you as you are about them.

This section suggests, in essence, that you consciously react to the behavior that constantly revolves about you during the school day—and that you consciously and constantly reflect on your reactions. Only then can you develop into a teacher who communicates a personality that pupils can examine critically and profitably during the school year. The next section will suggest ways in which you can do this.

HELP YOUR PUPILS UNDERSTAND YOU BETTER

It's generally quite interesting to watch elementary pupils meet their teachers in non-school surroundings. They seem surprised to discover that we attend films, shop in stores, go swimming, and even wear old clothes.

Since much of your effectiveness as an elementary teacher depends upon your ability to communicate the essence of your personality, do whatever you can to help your pupils know you as you really are. Help them discover interesting things about you all year long. Begin during the first days.

The First Days

Your pupils will be apprehensive about you the first day, so allay their fears by displaying all the warmth and humor you have within you. Greet them warmly, and let them know that you have prepared a place for them in your classroom and in your heart.

A cornball notion? Not at all. You have to really care about your pupils to teach them. And they'll know by the end of the first day whether or not your concern is genuine.

This is not to suggest that a warm welcome includes an invitation to unrestrained misbehavior on the part of your pupils. Rather, you should welcome them into a classroom that is the responsibility of a hard-working, concerned professional teacher who cares too much about his pupils to condone chaos. It is possible to be warm, friendly, kind, and humorous—and at the same time to be firm in your resolve to maintain a classroom environment in which pupils can learn comfortably, without turmoil. Chapter Nine suggests procedures you might follow in developing such an environment. The suggestions below deal with only one aspect of that larger problem—that is, with the intriguing task of helping your pupils discover whether or not you're worth knowing.

If you are teaching in a school where you can expect pupils to operate informally without an undue amount of restraint, you might set up informal displays to occupy their time as they arrive the first day. This will give them an opportunity to size up their classmates and you without being self-conscious about it. Let them find their homes on a map of the area. Let them work on a partially completed jigsaw puzzle on a table. Give them a dittoed sheet of paper with all the pupils' names and ask them to get the signatures of their classmates as they arrive. Display the books they will use during the year. Set out puzzles and games. Make the classroom gay and colorful. Play some soft music on the phonograph.

Forget about the butterflies in your stomach and concentrate on the butterflies in your pupils' stomachs. Communicate the competence and stability pupils (and their parents) hope to see when they meet their teachers for the first time. When the first school day officially begins, ask your pupils to go to their seats so you can get down to business. If you made the preliminaries interesting, the chances are good that your pupils will go along with your request, and the year will start off well.

Most teachers tell their pupils about themselves the first day. You might find it interesting and worthwhile to try something a bit more elaborate for a change.

Arrange a somewhat cryptic bulletin board display that merely hints at information about you and your interests. Use numbers, phrases, colors, pictures, shapes, and personal things you've collected through the years. Ask your class to guess what the various bits and pieces of the display mean as you unfold the story of your life the first day. A phrase such as "The Old Woman Who Lived in a Shoe" could suggest that you came from a large family. Many reds in the display could indicate that red is your favorite color. A picture of a house could depict your childhood home or your present home. A date could refer to your birth, your marriage, or your entry into the teaching profession. A drawing of a chicken could mean that chicken is your favorite food or that you like to draw. In each case, your pupils will enjoy guessing what the items in the display mean before you tell them—and they will begin to see you and think of you as a real person from the first day they meet you.

Another introductory device that uses a riddle format is a brief questionnaire that you can administer the second or third day of school, and then one month later. On it you would list questions about yourself such as: What is my favorite food? Where was I born? What is my hobby? What is my favorite color? How large a family do I come from? Do I like snow? etc. Ask your pupils to answer the questions as best they can after knowing you for only a couple of days. Gather the papers and file them away.

In the days that follow give clues to the answers to the questions you've asked in the questionnaire. Return the papers in a month and ask your pupils to respond to the items again, writing different answers wherever appropriate. Then give them the correct answers. In the discussion that follows, ask your pupils to tell how they discovered these things about you. You might be surprised to find out that you gave out far more clues than you thought you gave out—and you might also be surprised to find out that they discovered quite a few other things about you at the same time. It should be a lively discussion.

Slide-tape presentations are an excellent introductory device, and they really don't take as much effort as you might think. Another advantage is that a basic presentation can be used for several years, once it's developed. Make a series of slides that depict various aspects of your life—your childhood, your schooling, your present family situation and home. Arrange the slides in a sequence and tape record a narration to go with it. Whenever possible, add music, sound effects, and the actual voices of the people in the picture. Your pupils might enjoy hearing your parents' voices, especially if yours sounds similar to theirs. Consider including some pictures of highlights of the last school year to give your class a preview of experiences they might have this year.

Through the Year

Your pupils should discover interesting things about you all year long, and you can make this possible with very little effort. For example, invite a close friend or two to visit your room on occasion—during a party, to see something special your pupils did, or just whenever it's convenient to drop in for a bit. Your pupils know you as a teacher. They should also get to know you as an adult with interesting adult friends, and a life that extends beyond the confines of the classroom. If you are married, invite your spouse to visit school occasionally. Your pupils will observe you closely on such occasions, and they will learn much about you in the process. If you have a four or five year old child, you might bring him along to school once in a while. Your pupils will love to play with him and take care of him during the day—and again, they will have an excellent opportunity to observe you closely in a different role.

Don't hesitate to discuss the weekend and vacation periods with your pupils on Monday mornings, asking them what they did and telling them what you did. Throughout the year, share your joys and your sorrows with your pupils. Talk about books you've read, movies you saw, TV programs you enjoyed. You will, of course, always want to observe the dictates of good taste in such disclosures, and you will not want to bore your pupils by endlessly parading your life before them. Still, with relatively little effort, you will discover that you can weave much of yourself that is of interest to your class into all sorts of classroom activities.

FOUR

Observing Your Students

as a Group and as Individuals

*U*nbelievable as it might seem, the chances are good that two of your pupils have identical birthdays. Check your classroom and several others and be surprised. But while the laws of chance favor two identical birthdays in a classroom of at least 22 pupils, they won't predict who the two pupils will be, or on what day the two will celebrate their birthday. That's for you to discover.

The elementary school classroom is a living probability laboratory. Experienced teachers can predict many things that will happen during the school year—that mittens and baby teeth will be lost, and that new friends and garter snakes will be found, for example—but they can't predict when and to whom these things will happen. That's part of what makes classroom life so interesting—and sometimes so frustrating.

It's frustrating because while textbooks and teacher education courses tend to focus on the typical behavior of groups of pupils, teachers have to deal with the specific behavior of individual pupils. To illustrate, primary teachers are encouraged to change classroom activities every ten minutes or so because the attention span of a class of primary pupils is short. The fact is, though, that there is no such thing as a class attention span. Rather, there are many attention spans for each activity a class engages in, and it's this individual behavior that concerns the teacher.

Not that the ten minute suggestion has no merit. It has. Experienced primary teachers do tend to think in terms of ten or fifteen minute segments when planning a lesson. But they also realize that this time limitation is essentially little more than a convenient device that has evolved through all the experiences they've had with many groups of pupils engaged in many different activities. It's a good point at which to begin instructional planning. It's a theme on which they've learned to write endless variations.

Normative data is used widely in schools. It's used to determine class size, the scope and sequence of the curriculum, recommended instructional procedures, and even desk heights. The problem is that such data is only helpful to a point. It doesn't fit everyone. No matter what a teacher does in a classroom, the effect on individual pupils will vary. The activity that excites one pupil bores another. The assignment that is too difficult for one pupil is too easy for another. It's helpful to know how the typical pupil will respond to an activity or assignment or piece of furniture, but it's equally important to think beyond the elusive typical pupil to the special needs of each individual pupil.

You can't really fall back on your own experience as a child either to discover all the needs of the typical and individual pupil. Although all of us were once elementary pupils, none of us represents the elementary pupil of today. Each generation and individual in that generation contains elements of previous generations, but each also adds experiences that no previous generation had. Good times, bad times, wars, inventions, medical advances, new forms of communication—all these mark a generation and distinguish it from previous generations.

This suggests that you must constantly study your pupils to discover in them what is as new as today and as old as time— what is constant in all and unique in each. From such study comes the knowledge that will permit you to work effectively with your class as a group and with your pupils as individuals— to discover those things that will assist you in helping your pupils get the most out of school.

CONSIDER THE INVESTIGATIONS OF JEAN PIAGET

Even though your classroom study of pupils will be somewhat informal and limited, you can learn much by examining the methods and discoveries of eminent students of children's behavior. Jean Piaget is one such investigator. Piaget's clinical approach to child study, developed over a fifty year period, can be adapted by classroom teachers who are interested in increasing their understanding of the ways of children, and who are willing to make the effort to gain that knowledge.

Perhaps Piaget's major contribution was an extremely significant set of normative data on the intellectual development of children. It's a comprehensive picture that characterizes the child as the chief architect of his own intellectual growth. Each child develops in his own unique way, but within predictable boundaries identified and explored by Piaget.

Piaget investigated the intellectual development of children as a means of discovering (1) how man comes to know and use what he knows, and (2) how logic and thought are related. His studies, carried out in Geneva, Switzerland, have been published in over twenty books and in scores of articles and monographs, many of which have been translated into English. His findings have profoundly affected the structure and organization of the curriculum revision movement that characterizes elementary education today, and they have contributed to what we know about the social behavior of children. You can ill afford to be uninformed about Piaget and his work.

His Work

Piaget used a unique approach in his investigations. Initially, he followed his own children about and carefully observed their behavior and comments. Later, he expanded his investigations and standardized his procedures somewhat, but he continued to let children take the lead in exploring the situations and experiments he set before them.

He was always careful to question, observe, and record without distorting his subject's reactions. Piaget was not content to merely record answers to questions he asked of children. Rather, he let the children talk on their own accord, and he followed their lead, probing to find what was behind the obvious and superficial. Thus, he was able to get to the heart of children's thought and behavior.

Out of Piaget's careful efforts came a remarkably fresh view of the child and the procedures he uses to learn something and to respond to the world about him. A careful study of your pupils can likewise give you fresh insights into the behavior of children in a school setting.

His Ideas

Piaget discovered that learning is not merely a process of adding to previous knowledge. Rather, it is a dynamic and continual mental reorganization that draws on maturation, prior experience, and language factors in its search for equilibration. Equilibration is the balanced relationship that develops as a person assimilates the outside world into himself, and at the same time accommodates himself to the demands of the outside world. A young reader, confronted with an unfamiliar word, will assimilate its existence and configuration into his mind; then he will accommodate himself to the adjustments he will make in his reading rhythm as he stops to sound out the word. The experience may well lead to the mastery of a new word that he will be able to read without pause the next time he sees it.

Learning is a slow process because the outside world can only be assimilated into our minds at a rate previous assimilation will permit. Each new bit of data from the outside world must be related to something similar that has already been assimilated, and these two are then reorganized into a larger meaning. Thus, the process of assimilation makes the unfamiliar familiar; it makes the new old—and this takes time.

Piaget suggests that the child goes through four main stages in his mental development. The rate of progress will vary from child to child, but the boundaries Piaget establishes for each stage provide a useful set of categories for teachers since they tend to work with groups of youngsters.

The Sensory-Motor Stage occupies approximately the first two years of the child's life. The child has few movements at birth, and these tend to be of the reflex type—swallowing, sucking, moving his tongue. During the next two years, though, he will add many movements to his initial repertoire until he will be able to make such advanced movements as crawling around to the other side of an object he's pushed to a wall so that he can continue pushing it some more. During this stage he develops the basic practical knowledge that serves as the structure of his future experiences with the outside world.

The Preoperational Representations Stage takes the child through the first grade or so. During this period he begins to establish relationships between experience and action, to manipulate language and symbols. He does this primarily by imitating models and by accommodating his behavior to the behavior he observes in others.

This stage is also characterized by the things the child can't do. He can't distinguish clearly between external reality and internal motives. He thinks the sun pushes the clouds and the rain falls because people have put on their raincoats. He also can't grasp the concept of reversability. When the shape of a clay object is changed into something else, he will not suggest that it can be readily brought back to its original shape. When a volume of water is poured from a squat container into a tall thin container of equal volume, he will suggest that the taller container contains more water.

The Concrete Operations Stage covers the elementary school years essentially, and so it is of special interest to us. Piaget sees the idea of an operation as being central to the development of knowledge. Knowledge is not a copy of reality. You have to be able to act on an object, to modify it, to transform it, to know how it is put together—if you truly want to understand it.

Compared with his pre-school brother, the elementary school child has developed a more adequate system of dealing with the outside world. He can better explore the present on the basis of the past. His ability to deal with concrete operations is a significant part of this difference. He no longer has to handle an object to deal with it. He can internalize it—carry out activities with it within his mind. He can count its parts without touching them. He can mentally arrange a series of objects in order from the largest to the smallest. He can classify a set of similar objects.

An operation is also reversible, and elementary school children learn to handle many reversible actions. They understand that if they divide a plate of fudge into pieces, they can restore the original quantity by returning all the pieces to the plate. In school they add and subtract, join and separate objects, construct and tear down. Through such experiences they can help prepare themselves for the hypothetical activities that constitute mature thought.

The Formal Operations Stage begins at about junior high school age when the child develops the capacity to operate on hypothetical propositions rather than be bound by things that are right before his face. At this point the child can think through a full set of alternatives to a simple problem and select the most sensible procedure. In short, he has learned to think logically and abstractly.

Your Challenge

And so the child has developed from a breathing but almost helpless body into a smoothly functioning intellect. What role can the school play in this process?

Piaget sees the school's role as one of tying into and enriching the normal development of the child as much as possible. This suggests that you give serious consideration to the following two proposals.

First, make curricular and instructional decisions with the child's developmental stages in mind. Suppose your pupils are in the Concrete Operations Stage. Among other things, this would suggest that they should have many opportunities to perform real actions on real objects instead of just reading or hearing about how others did it. The newer science programs are good illustrations of such curricular planning. Several have dispensed completely with textbooks, and the rest have reduced printed materials for pupils to a bare minimum. The programs focus on activities in which pupils actually work with science materials, discovering firsthand what previous generations only read about in textbooks.

Take a good hard look at what you're doing this week. How many things will you do that your pupils could profitably do? For starters, could they design your bulletin board displays, keep attendance records, take the lunch count, run the projector, alphabetize papers, and run the ditto machine? Obviously, you can do each of these tasks more efficiently than your pupils can, but ask yourself whether or not it wouldn't be better for your pupils to take over as many activities as possible in which they actually handle and manipulate objects and devices. It is only through such manipulative experiences that pupils grow in their ability to deal with the world about them.

Or, how often do you rely on words in your teaching when it is possible to teach your pupils by letting them actually manipulate objects? Look at the square and the rectangle in Figure 1. The square measures 8 units by 8 units, or 64 units.

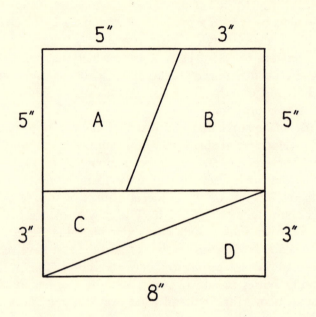

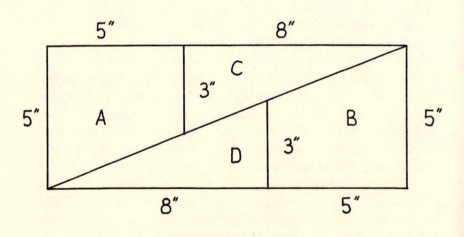

FIGURE 1

Cut up the square as shown, rearrange it into the rectangular form, and it becomes 13 units by 5 units, or 65 square units. Where did the extra square unit come from?

It would be possible to explain this phenomenon with words, but your pupils wouldn't really understand it. The only way a person will ever understand what happened is to take a good sized sheet of paper, mark it off, cut it up, and arrange it in the square and rectangular forms. Careful examination will lead to the discovery of the extra square unit (spread out along the diagonal line), and it will also teach your pupils important things about angles that words alone can't teach. Try it and see.

Second, make decisions about the organization and management of your classroom with the child's developmental stages in mind. Elementary pupils should become involved in group activities that free them from their egocentrism and get them to interact with each other. They should be placed into situations in which they examine their behavior and the results of their behavior, so they can begin to see their behavior as an important part of the learning activities that constitute their school's curriculum.

Playground behavior provides many such opportunities. Teachers typically are irritated by squabbles that begin during a play period and continue as pupils return to their classroom —with a half dozen pupils shouting accusations at each other and another equally loud group of eyewitnesses trying to clarify the situation at the same time.

Don't become irritated with such behavior. It defines your immediate task. If they knew how to settle their squabble by themselves, they wouldn't have brought it to you. Get everyone settled and go to work on it as a group. Observations must be reported and inferences made. Both sides (or all sides) must be heard, and so articulate and persuasive presentations must be made. Evidence and opinion must be weighed, conclusions drawn. Think. What could you possibly do during that period that would be more important than settling the argument? Your pupils should grow through such deliberate activity, frustrating though it will be at first. The chaos of the fall months should give way to more reasoned and reasonable argumentation in winter. And who knows, by spring your pupils may have learned something that many nations (that only shout and fight) have yet to learn!

Piaget's work should also encourage you to dig more deeply into the many explorations that have been made of children's development. Piaget is but one of many serious students who have contributed to our knowledge of child behavior.

But don't forget that you must also balance this general knowledge of normative data on pupils that others have gathered with specific knowledge that you gather on your own classroom full of pupils. Let's turn to that task next.

BEGIN IN THE FILE FOLDERS

You first meet your pupils in the file cabinet. There, a pupil's previous teachers have compressed him and his school experiences into a few letters, numbers, symbols, and comments.

Properly interpreted, these evaluations can prove invaluable—especially during the early weeks of the school year—since each entry represents information some teacher considered important enough to pass on. Unfortunately, several factors combine to make it difficult to interpret file entries. Let's examine these factors and then seek solutions.

One problem is that space limitations force teachers to fit many different kinds of specific evaluations into a few general categories. Thus, a C grade can be used to report the extent of a pupil's mastery of the multiplication tables, but it can also be used to evaluate the quality of his participation in a group project that investigates community recreational opportunities. In evaluating the first instance, the end product —a thorough mastery of the multiplication tables—is generally considered more important than the memorization processes used. In evaluating the second instance, the processes the pupils use in working together are generally considered more important than the end product—their findings.

Each evaluation a teacher enters into the file at the end of the year represents an accumulated evaluation of many different kinds of activities. The result of this combining is that the next teacher has no way of knowing precisely what a grade such as a C in a given curricular or behavioral area might mean. It could mean that the pupil was average in everything, or that he did well in one kind of activity and poorly in another, or that effort or achievement or even neatness counted more than other things, or that some other formula was used to arrive at the final letter (or number or check mark) evaluation. The symbol itself won't tell you. You'll have to seek explanations in comments that accompany the grades.

But here also you may run into problems. It's often difficult to distinguish between observations and inferences in teacher's comments. An observation is knowledge gained directly through any of the senses—that a pupil frequently falls asleep during school, for example. An inference is a conclusion developed on the basis of information observed—that the pupil is tired during the day because his parents argue late into the night. Such an inference might be right or wrong. File folders frequently contain such short general statements without the supporting data that would make the information helpful. If you have any reason to doubt the correctness of an inference, it's better to suspend judgment until you've had an opportunity to meet the pupil yourself, or at least to get additional information.

Actually, it's not a bad idea to suspend judgment on much of the evaluative material you'll find in file folders until you've had an opportunity to work with your pupils. Some educators even suggest that teachers should stay away from the file folders until they've had a chance to meet their pupils without prejudice.

That's probably going a bit far. A pre-school examination of file folders can accomplish several important things, even with all the difficulties in interpretation described above.

Although specific evaluations might often be meaningless, class and individual patterns do evolve and these can prove quite meaningful. For example, you might discover that the grades your pupils received last year tended to be higher or lower than the grades they had received in previous years, or than their intelligence and achievement test scores would pre- dict. This might suggest that your pupils were pushed too hard or not hard enough last year, or that something else was awry. In any event, you should do some additional checking on what happened before school begins. It's quite possible that you'll have a difficult group to work with during the first few weeks of the school year. You'll probably find it advisable to arrange things so that they can evaluate much of their own work during September, and you'll certainly spend time dis- cussing the nature and function of classroom evaluation with them.

A somewhat common example of a pattern evolving in an individual pupil's file folder is that of a consistently negative evaluation on school behavior. Follow up such cases. Contact former teachers and others who can give additional informa- tion. Especially seek out anyone who might have had a bit of success in reaching the pupil. It's quite possible that the first few days of the school year will be critical in your relationship with such a pupil. A few hours spent on the case in August could save hours upon hours of effort through the year.

As you work through the files, jot down your reactions to what you see. Don't rely on your memory. In general, what kind of a class is it? What kinds of homes do the pupils come from? Can you expect parents to support or work against the things you plan to do? What kinds of experiences have your pupils had? What problems are apparent? What approaches to solving these problems suggest themselves? What things seem to interest the pupils? Can you begin the year drawing heavily on their interests and strengths?

Examining pupil records during August won't answer all these questions or solve all your problems in September. Actu- ally, the chances are good that you won't even have files avail- able on all your pupils, or that the entries won't be consistently helpful. Nevertheless, you'd be foolish to meet your class with anything less than all the information you can possibly get—whether it be from the files, former teachers, the principal, the nurse, the custodian, or others who know the pupils you will work with. You can learn something of value from almost all the information you can get.

It's unfortunate that you'll often have to wade through quite a bit of vague and immaterial data to find the really significant items—but that's the way things often are. Don't lose heart, though. Those few significant items might well make a big difference in getting the school year off to a good start, so they're worth going after.

GET ACQUAINTED EARLY WITH ALL YOUR PUPILS

Even a careful pre-school examination of pupil records won't prepare you completely for the first day confusion of meeting an entire class at once. The chances are that you will (almost of necessity) concentrate your attention initially on the vigorous outgoing pupils and on those who deliberately seek your attention, and it might even be some time before you really get to know the quieter, unassuming pupils.

Try not to let this happen. The quieter pupils need your attention as much as the noisier ones—perhaps even more. Seek ways in which you can get to know all your pupils during the first days of the school year.

Activities in which pupils write about themselves are especially good because you don't have to respond immediately, and so there is no competition for your immediate attention. You can examine what they have to say at length during the more contemplative after school hours. Written information-seeking activities generally take two forms: a free response essay-type paper in which pupils write autobiographical information about themselves, and a dittoed interest inventory in which pupils respond to specific questions about themselves such as: My favorite food is ____, My hobby is ____, TV programs I watch are ____.

With a little imagination you can develop many interesting and useful variations on these two basic activities, and these should give you quite a bit of background information on your pupils. Work them into your language arts program. Use a tape recorder with younger pupils and with others who may have difficulty writing about their experiences. Ask them to go to the listening table sometime during the day and tape their comments and stories. It really doesn't make much difference whether you read what they have written or listen to what they have said.

Write a number of words on the chalkboard and ask your pupils to respond with a sentence or paragraph in which they describe an experience they have had with the term, or to indicate if they haven't had any experience with the term. For example, you might use such words as: cows, ocean, birthday party, airplane, camping, public library, restaurant, bus, rats, ball, friend, fun. Select terms that will figure in school activities you have planned in the near future, and then in your class activities build on the experiences your pupils have had.

Duplicate a short story (or parallel stories for boys and girls) in which you describe a series of experiences a child the age of your pupils might have had. Ask your pupils to read the story and underline all the things that have also happened to them. Then ask them to expand on one or two of their experiences in some detail. Your story might begin something like this:

> Billy was very happy when his mother said they were going shopping downtown. He always liked to ride on the city buses. It was raining lightly and he held the umbrella on the way to the bus stop. While they were waiting for the bus to come, a fire started in a building across the street. Someone ran out and turned in the alarm, and soon fire engines arrived. . . .

Short-term diaries can provide a wealth of information on pupils, if handled properly. Tell your pupils that you are learning to know them quite well in school, but that you realize they do many interesting and important things out of school that relate to school experiences. The first thing every morning for a week or so ask them to write what they did from the time school ended yesterday until they went to bed. They should concentrate on the more important things that occurred. Emphasize that diaries are meant to be confidential, so you will not repeat anything specifically that anyone writes—but that they might enjoy a report on the common experiences they had —the TV shows the class watched, what they had for supper, when they went to bed, etc. Such a general report could lead to an interesting and informative class discussion. Many pupils need to discover that their normal activities are really quite interesting. You can help them see richness in their lives if you exhibit genuine enthusiasm for the experiences they have. If a pupil tells you one day he's going to see his aunt and uncle that evening, ask about it the next morning. Talk about the TV shows they watch, the films they see. Be interested in their lives.

The activities described above ask pupils to respond to questions you initiate. You can also learn much about them by examining the questions they raise. To illustrate, on Monday you might ask your pupils to write down several questions they would like answered before the week is over. Collect their questions and lay them aside. At the end of the week return their papers and ask them to put an X in front of each question that was answered during the week. Gather in the papers again, and study them over the weekend to see what kinds of questions your pupils want answered, your ability to perceive them, and the extent to which the school activities you plan meet the needs they express. Be sure to answer all the unanswered questions early the following week—and then discuss with them ways in which they can communicate problems and questions to you.

One simple way to assess the strengths and interests of your pupils early in the year is to ask them to code all the written work they hand in. They should place a 1, 2, or 3 *and* an A, B, or C at the bottom of each paper. *1,* I found this assignment very difficult. *2,* I found this assignment challenging but not too difficult. *3,* I found this assignment easy. *A,* I enjoy this type of assignment very much. *B,* I am neutral about this type of assignment. *C,* I do not like this type of assignment. This coding device (or some variation on it) will help you adjust class work to the abilities and interests of your pupils.

Even though written activities such as the ones described above can give you much information about your pupils, you will probably have more opportunities to get to know your pupils through the many informal personal and class discussions that characterize classroom life. Keep your eyes and ears especially alert for those moments when your pupils might want to share part of themselves with you—a dream, an idea, a concern, a bit of their background. When such moments occur, drop whatever else you are doing and hear the pupil out. The opportunity might not arise again. Always have several interesting general activities for occasions such as this—something you can quickly use that will occupy your class while you work with such a pupil.

Try to arrange class activities during the early weeks of the school year so you'll be able to spend at least fifteen or twenty minutes talking informally with each of your pupils. Use odd moments before and after school, during study periods, and during periods when pupils are doing seatwork. Don't give the impression of a formally scheduled interview. Rather, use some event, question, or problem that involves the pupil as a place to begin a conversation that will help the two of you get better acquainted. Listen mostly. Talk mainly to get the pupil talking about himself and the things he has done and would like to do.

One of the best ways to get to know a pupil is to observe him carefully when he is relatively free to do anything he wants to do. Give your pupils many such opportunities early in the year, and then watch carefully to see what they do—to see who reads, who draws, who builds, who socializes, who daydreams, who disturbs others.

Experienced teachers know that a few minutes spent with parents can often clear up many minor questions they have about a pupil. Unfortunately, PTA meetings and open house sessions aren't conducive to such discussions, and teachers hesitate to ask parents to come to school for a series of minor questions. The telephone can be a good solution to this problem if you find it easy to chat informally on the phone. Call evenings after your pupils are in bed. Set the parent at ease immediately, using a pretext of telling something good the pupil did that day if necessary. Then lead into the questions you wanted to ask. Encourage the parent to ask questions too, or to move the discussion into other areas he would like to discuss.

SEEK HELP FOR SPECIAL PROBLEMS

Most class groups seem to have at least one pupil with serious behavior problems, and many classes have several. Perhaps the most important thing for you to realize is that your preparation for teaching didn't really prepare you properly to deal with such problems. There is no need to apologize. Your preparation was essentially normative—concerned with the problems of teaching groups of pupils within the normal behavior and intelligence range. Extreme deviations generally require special preparation and much individual attention from a teacher. And although many teachers develop such competencies over the years, most still realize that they can accomplish more by working with specialists than they can by going it alone.

Guidance and counseling services at the elementary and junior high levels have increased considerably in recent years. The chances are good that you have such services available to you, either through your local or intermediate district, or through county and state agencies. Private agencies also exist in some localities. Find out what is available, and then draw on those resources best suited to your problem.

Severe behavior problems are generally evident almost from the beginning of the school year. They can take several forms—behavior that is *unusually:* loud and disruptive, quiet and withdrawn, emotionally erratic, argumentative, interested in sexuality, immature, etc. The key word is *unusually*. What may seem unusual to you might be within the normal range of behavior to others (and vice versa).

So your first task is to examine past records of pupils whose behavior might be considered very unusual. How did former teachers see these pupils? Is there any information in such pupils' records that would help you understand their situations better?

Next, begin to gather your own data on these pupils' behavior. Perhaps the best way to do this is to keep behavior diaries. Involve the pupils in individual and group situations in which they will react in ways that will help you understand their behavior. Walk with them when the class is going to the lunchroom or playground. Ask them to write stories about themselves during language arts lessons. Place them into positions of temporary leadership and responsibility. Observe carefully during all these activities and record your reactions. Be sure also to ask yourself honestly whether you personally dislike any of these pupils, and whether or not your feelings intensify the pupil's behavior and thus cloud the situation. Inquire also into the pupils' home situations. How do these pupils see their homes? How do their parents see the situation? How do former teachers see it?

Once you have done your homework on these situations, you are in a good position to be of help when you and the counselor sit down to discuss a problem and plan the action that should be taken.

Your major role after referral is to follow the program you and the counselor set up for dealing with the pupil, and to report on progress or lack of progress. If the program doesn't work, develop another course of action together. Don't go off in opposite directions.

And don't expect a miracle solution to a complex problem either. Many of these problems involve family and environmental factors that are beyond the scope of the school to solve. Essentially, your task is to administer first aid in such situations, to try to communicate to the pupil that, regardless of his life out of school, the people who work with him during school hours love him for what he is, and will do their best to provide a pleasant place for him to learn.

The only way you can communicate this, though, is to really believe it, and to practice it.

EXAMINE THE SOCIAL CLIMATE OF YOUR CLASSROOM

Any study of your pupils should include an investigation of the social climate of the classroom. The sociogram is a common device for beginning such a study. It can help you identify class leaders, isolates, cliques, and potential friendships, and it can also help you assess the general cohesiveness of the class. It normally cannot tell you how intense the relationships are, how influential individual pupils are with their classmates, and why pupils made the choices they made.

A sociogram is quite easy to construct. It is essentially nothing more than an arrangement of small groups within the class based on the pupils' choices of partners or friends. Begin by asking your pupils to identify and rank three pupils they would like to work with or sit near; or you might merely ask them to rank their three best friends or three classmates they admire. Each pupil should write his choices on a slip of paper, placing his own name in the upper right hand corner. Write all the pupils' names on the chalkboard so spelling won't cause a problem and absent pupils won't be forgotten.

Collect the slips of paper and insert the choices in a form similar to the one in Figure 2. In the illustration Bill's first choice is Tom, his second choice is Frank, and his third choice is Sam. When all the pupils' choices are entered, indicate the number of first, second, and third choices each pupil received at the bottom of the form, as illustrated in Figure 2.

The sociogram can be drawn in a number of ways. In Figure 3, boys' names are placed in boxes and girls' names in circles. Examine choices to determine the best placement of names. It's generally best to place the most frequently chosen pupils in the center of the sociogram, and mutual choices near each other. Draw an arrow from the pupil doing the selecting to the pupil selected. Write a 1, 2, or 3 near the arrowhead

	BILL	FRANK	JOHN	SAM	TOM	LOIS	MARY	NANCY	SARAH	SUE
BILL		2		3	1					
FRANK	1				2	3				
JOHN	1	3		2						
SAM	1				2	3				
TOM	1	3		2						
LOIS		3					2			1
MARY							2	3		1
NANCY	3					2	1			
SARAH	1	3		2						
SUE					3	2	1			
1ST CHOICE	5	0	0	0	1	0	2	0	0	2
2ND CHOICE	0	1	0	3	2	3	1	0	0	0
3RD CHOICE	1	4	0	1	1	2	0	1	0	0

FIGURE 2

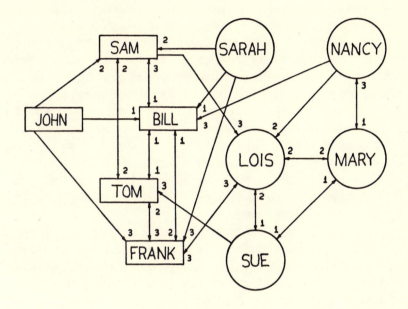

FIGURE 3

to indicate first, second, or third choice. Indicate mutual choices with a double-headed arrow.

Study the sociogram to discover social patterns within the group. In the sociogram in Figure 3, John and Sarah are isolates, selected by no one. Bill is the most popular boy. He was also selected by two girls, but these girls are unpopular with the other girls. Lois received the most choices among the girls, but none were first choices. Lois, Mary, and Sue form a group that Nancy would like to join. Mary seems to be the key to her acceptance (unless Mary chose her third as the best of three evils: Nancy, Sarah, or a boy). Sarah either dislikes all four girls very much, or else she has just discovered boys. The girls are more interested in boys than the boys are in girls. Only Mary didn't choose a boy, while only Frank and Sam chose a girl—Lois, who also chose Frank.

This sample group had only ten pupils. Your larger class group would contain many more interesting relationships that would raise questions you should try to answer. Consider just a few of the questions the findings above raise. How can John achieve acceptance? Why did Sarah reject all four girls and why did they reject her? Do Sam and Frank dislike each other because of Lois, or is it just that each likes Lois better? Does this group exhibit as much cohesiveness as can be expected?

If you asked your pupils to identify classmates they would like to work with on a committee, or sit near in a seating re-arrangement, then you are morally committed to honor their choices. You should tell them in advance, of course, that you will not be able to give everyone his first choice, but that you will honor as many wishes as possible. That's why you are asking them to list three choices.

Follow these general principles in selecting groups. Honor the wishes of isolates or near isolates first. Don't place more than one or two isolates in any group since they don't usually mix well with each other. Place each pupil with at least one of his choices. Where pair relationships are indicated, give a pupil his highest reciprocated choice.

Even though constructing and interpreting a sociogram can take a bit of your time, it's time well spent. It's too easy to assume that the pupils you like best are also best liked by their classmates, or to underestimate the acceptance of the poor student or the quiet student. Developing sociograms at regular intervals (based on different questions) can give you a more accurate picture of the relationships within your class than you can get in any other way. But a sociogram is only as good as the questions you ferret out of it—and the effort and imagination you put into the solution of these questions.

LOOK BEHIND YOUR TESTS AND EXERCISES

The class testing program is perhaps the most constant and conspicuous medium you have for studying your pupils. Much of your out-of-class time is spent constructing, correcting, and interpreting the many different kinds of tests and exercises you administer to your pupils. Even though most elementary school textbook, teacher-made, and standardized tests are generally oriented around academic achievement, you can learn many other things about your pupils through them.

The achievement test provides a good illustration. Suppose a fourth grade pupil you had working in a third grade reader scored 4.6 in reading in an achievement test. Would your reaction be that the test was too easy, that he was lucky in guessing answers, or that he had cheated? Most of us would dismiss the score as inaccurate and forget about it.

The fact is, though, that the score might be completely accurate. Most pupils do their very best during achievement tests. Even a pupil with relatively poor concentration habits can usually concentrate well for the twenty minutes a test takes. The result is that he might do far better than he would do during a typical reading lesson. He might not be able to continue the pace his test scores indicate, but his test performance does indicate the heights he can reach—properly motivated and taught. The 4.6 represents your challenge, and not a score to dismiss lightly.

Why do tests generally create an atmosphere of greater concentration in a classroom than do other kinds of classroom activity? A good classroom discussion often won't actively involve more than half of the class at any given moment, but even a poorly constructed test will usually occupy the undivided attention of most of the pupils. Explore this phenomenon with your pupils. Focus the discussion on their behavior during tests and during other kinds of classroom activities.

You might lead into this by examining a selection of recent tests and exercises you gave them. Reproduce a few test and workbook pages on overhead transparencies. Examine them item by item with your class to see if they can discover what captured and held their attention. Were some questions more challenging than others? Were some tests and exercises better than others? Why?

A good test item should be directly relevant to a course

objective that was clearly communicated to the class. It should focus specifically on the pupil's progress towards that objective. It should permit easy and accurate interpretation. It should encourage an answer that can be easily and accurately interpreted.

What all of this says is that tests are essentially a form of compact communication between teacher and pupil and between pupil and teacher. Thus, their intent is similar to any class activity. The difference, as pupils see it and respond to it, is that the test is more important than the typical lesson. Teachers spend more time and effort constructing, correcting, and interpreting tests than they do in preparing for typical lessons. Teachers base much of their report card grading on test performance.

What the teacher considers important the pupils will consider important. And so the pupil is apt to concentrate his attention on an achievement test and daydream during a typical reading lesson. What the 4.6 pupil reading in a third grade reader is trying to say to his teacher is that he can do better, and he is willing to do better under the right circumstances.

But you'll never know he's trying to tell you that if you won't look behind the superficial aspects of classroom life. To understand your pupils, you have to study them as continuously and intensely as they study you. And that's quite a bit.

FIVE

Creating a Wholesome and

Attractive School Environment

We are all transients in our own schools. Every institution has a life of its own that is independent of the people who inhabit it at any given time. Any of us could drop dead in an evening and someone else would be teaching our class the following morning. Any of our pupils could move away over a weekend and his classroom space would be re-assigned the following week.

Such departures are noted. We talk about good-old-so-and-so and recall his idiosyncracies for a while, but in time new challenges and new faces that don't involve the departed come to the fore, and eventually all of us become little more than a hazy part of the tradition that springs up around an institution. Attend Homecoming Week five years after you've graduated from college. Return to your childhood neighborhood or church and talk with old friends who remained there. It won't take you five minutes to discover that you're out of things, even though the institution itself is as alive as it was when you helped make it live.

A morbid view? Not at all. While we inhabit an institution, we *are* the institution. It's ours! We breathe life into it. We help shape it. We add to its tradition. But when we leave it, we are no longer an active part of it. Others take over, and that's how it should be. The institution exists to serve its present inhabitants.

Institutions shouldn't become so bogged down with the specter of past glories and decisions that the present is stifled. "We'll do what we've always done." "That's not the way we did it last year." "It's always been traditional to . . ." are statements through which the small-minded, the unimaginative, and the fearful try to call upon the authority of the departed to add strength to a weak position.

The past should guide, but it should not dictate the present course of an institution. Trouble begins when the present staff and student body of a school feel that they are little more than intruders in someone else's school with no real sense of ownership, with no responsibility to chart its present course. Witness the recent period of unrest on college and university campuses. Students don't generally vandalize their own property.

The worst thing you can do to an institution is to sap the sense of ownership and responsibility the present inhabitants should have. The most important contribution you can make to an institution is to help it evolve into something that demands that each new generation of inhabitants takes the responsibility for full ownership.

Let's explore ways in which staff and pupils can work together in your school to create the sort of wholesome environment an institution needs to remain vigorous.

BEGIN WITH DESKS

Little variation was built into many housing developments constructed in the late 1940's. Developers uprooted trees and leveled the terrain. They generally used only about a half dozen essentially similar house plans, and they placed the houses on identical rectangular lots. Drive through such a development today, though, and you will see how many homeowners used painting, landscaping, and additions to make their houses unique—even though the developers seemingly did all they could to discourage it. Step inside those homes and you will see even more individuality.

Faculty offices in colleges and universities tend to be standardized in size and equipment. Walk down a hall and look into the offices, however, and you will see considerable variation (at least in their disorder).

Secretaries in large secretarial pools have identical desks and equipment. And even though some firms prohibit adornment, you will still find many individualistic touches on the desks.

But why talk of others? Look at the pictures, tools, and mementos that adorn *your* desk and make it unique.

Man's drive for individuality runs deep. We want a bit of space we can call our own, and we want others to recognize it as ours—as something that communicates our individuality to others. Is it surprising then that elementary school pupils have the same desire to make their desks uniquely theirs?

It's a small matter, perhaps, but we can draw on that desire as we attempt to develop a sense of responsible institutional membership in pupils. If encouraging them to transform their standardized desks into spaces that bear their unique stamps of ownership helps do the job of getting pupils to identify with their school, go to it.

The typical elementary school classroom allows for about 35 sq. ft. of space per pupil. In many classrooms desks are arranged in rows so that each pupil's space and desk resemble the housing developments described above—and often with the same depressing results. Let's look at the space and personal needs of an elementary classroom and its pupils and see how these needs can be met through seating patterns that give each pupil a space he feels is uniquely his.

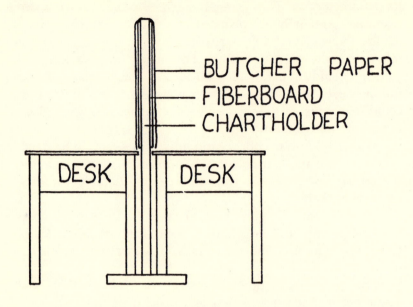

FIGURE 4-A

We might consider three needs. First, each pupil should have a space that is his, that he can feel free to arrange and to decorate. Second, this space should allow for a bit of privacy when he is doing individual work. Third, the total seating arrangement should permit easy transition between individual and group activities.

One simple and very effective solution to these three needs is to transform the desks into simple carrels that are placed around the perimeter of the room. This arrangement frees the center of the room for group activities.

You can easily make carrels for two or four pupils. Figures 4-A and 4-B show two views of a four-pupil carrel constructed from two two-pupil desks arranged to face each other. The divider between the desks can be easily adapted from a chartholder, or it can be constructed from readily obtainable materials with little effort. It should be about five feet high, and as wide as the

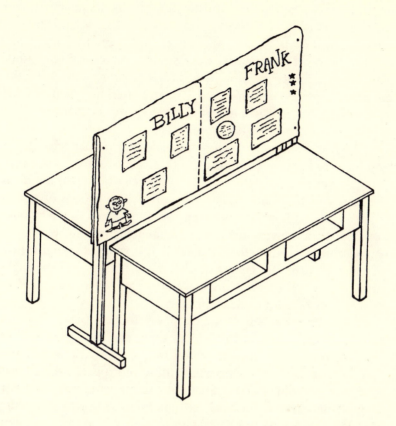

FIGURE 4-B

desks it screens. Use fiberboard covered with colored butcher paper for the screened area. Butcher paper makes a good surface since it can be easily changed. Encourage pupils to write or draw on their divider, to pin or staple pictures on it, and in general to decorate it in any way that will please them.

Experience has shown that this arrangement has several advantages over conventional seating arrangements. First, since the divider is an extension of the desk and lends itself to decoration, the pupil develops a sense of desk ownership that generally doesn't occur with conventional desk arrangements. Second, teachers report that pupils with this desk arrangement feel no need to mark on their desk tops, and that they tend to keep their desks neater. Third, the carrel arrangement lends itself especially well to individual work since it removes distractions. In a four-pupil carrel a pupil has direct contact only with the pupil sitting next to him, and he can't even see many of his classmates. Pupils who can't work well sitting next to someone else can be assigned to two-pupil carrels.

Figure 5 shows a room arrangement using carrels. When you want to bring your pupils together for a discussion or other group activity, ask them to move their chairs into a circle in the center of the room. When you want small groups of pupils to work around tables, just remove the carrel dividers temporarily. In a conventional room arrangement, empty space is spread thinly around the outside of the room. Concentrating all this space in the center of the room makes a surprisingly large area of space constantly available for activities that formerly required a lot of desk shifting.

Creating carrels isn't the only way to help pupils develop a sense of pride and ownership in their desks, of course. And actually, carrels are inappropriate in some situations and impossible in others. The important thing to do is to take a good hard look at your specific situation. Think imaginatively. For example, let them make small personal banners or flags to hang from their desks. Arrange desks in clusters and encourage each group to create identifying decorations for their set of desks. Some teachers set aside a few minutes each week so their pupils can clean out their desks and wash off the surfaces. One class arranged a tongue-in-cheek "Tour of Desks" similar to a tour of homes that was being held in their community. Several pupils who had unusually interesting (?) arrangements of books and things in their desks displayed their desks. Admission to the tour was a fall flower that went into a bouquet that helped beautify the room that week. Ridiculous? Perhaps—but activities such as these suggest that with a little humor and imagination your pupils can begin to think of their desks *as theirs.* That's one of several starting points for accepting the responsibilities of institutional membership, so it's worth going after.

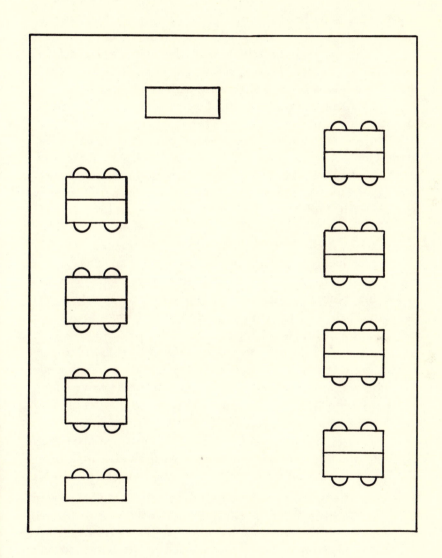

FIGURE 5

BREATHE LIFE INTO YOUR CLASSROOM

Don't underestimate the positive emotional impact your classroom can have on your pupils' behavior. It's the place your pupils usually think of when they tell their parents they're off to school. It's perhaps the one place away from home where they feel they can leave their belongings without undue fear of loss. It's the part of the school with the most clearly defined sense of community. "It's mine." "It's ours!" Build on these factors and you can work effectively with emotion-laden values that play a significant role in determining pupil behavior patterns.

Two sets of factors affect the emotional climate of a classroom. One set includes factors that remain somewhat constant, and so generally have a moderate but constant emotional effect upon the class because pupils know what to expect and they prepare for it. Heat, light, acoustics, furniture, and the amount of available space are examples of this set of factors. The other set of factors is characterized by sudden change, and these factors generally have a more noticeable emotional effect upon pupils because they don't know what to expect. Sudden changes in weather, power failures, unusual noise or activity outside the classroom, behavioral outbursts, and radical changes in routine are examples of this set of factors.

Both sets of factors can cause problems in classroom behavior and relationships—especially if you don't anticipate the problems and don't arrange things to lessen the negative effects of the situation. Jostling is common in crowded classrooms, and cloakroom confusion seems inevitable on a rainy day.

Don't let such problems discourage you, because they really help define your challenge as a teacher—that of preparing children to live effectively in a democratic society. Situations such as these can be turned into excellent learning experiences for your pupils. Consider the two illustrations above—a crowded classroom, and confusion in the cloakroom. They parallel, at the classroom level, real problems that larger society faces: (1) overcrowded cities, and (2) the confusion that a sudden weather change can cause (taxis, no umbrellas, snow removal, wind damage, etc.).

Face such problems squarely, and involve your pupils in their solution. After all, the problems involve your pupils too. So often we give lip service to pupil involvement in school decision-making, and so often this involvement focuses on nothing more important than the preferred flavor to use in the punch at a room party. These real and significant problems can provide far more exciting challenges for your pupils.

Constant Factors

Suppose your classroom is crowded, and that this is causing behavior problems. Scolding your pupils and wishing you had a larger classroom won't solve your immediate problem. Attacking the essence of the problem might, though, and it should help develop a sympathetic understanding of the situation on the part of your pupils anyway.

Ask each of your pupils to observe classroom interaction for a week and to keep a record of problems that arose because the room was crowded. Collect their records at the end of the week and ask a committee of pupils to examine them—to see if they can discover common patterns, things of significance. Did many problems tend to arise on some days and few on others, at some specific times of the day and not at others? What other factors were present when problems arose? Did all pupils report essentially the same problem situations or did different pupils see the situations differently? Did problems tend to occur in some parts of the room and not in others? The committee might want to develop charts and graphs that indicate when and where trouble arises. A spirited class discussion should follow their report.

Seek solutions. If problems arise when the room becomes too warm or stuffy, try to work out a better way to control temperature and air circulation. If pupils brush each other as they move about the room, create a Traffic Commission and/or Zoning Commission to explore ways of rearranging traffic patterns and seating arrangements in the room. What about one-way aisles? What about some narrow aisles and some wider aisles with most traffic channeled down the wider aisles? What about belt-line or perimeter traffic? What about placing the desks close together in one section of the room in order to get a wider expanse of open space in another area? Can work areas in the classroom be screened from study areas? Can some furniture be removed from the room? Can the corridor and patio be used more than they are presently used? Note how these questions parallel the kinds of questions city officials ask as they wrestle with the problems of inadequate living space in an urban setting.

Fluctuating Factors

Involve your pupils also in handling the behavior problems caused by sudden environmental changes. A surprising number of these can be anticipated—a coming storm, a maintenance crew working outside the classroom, the movement of other classes down the corridor outside your classroom. Let your pupils know when to expect such things, and discuss what adjustments you might make when the situations occur. A simple adjustment in the sequence of the day's activities might eliminate the distraction a jackhammer might cause, for example. Jackhammers can really disrupt an oral reading lesson, but they might add a bit of spice to an art or P.E. activity.

When unexpected things occur, be as curious as your pupils. Go outside or to the window together and watch it for a few minutes, then return to what you were doing (if what you were doing really is more interesting and important).

Think beyond the immediate problems that arise, and concentrate some of your energies on all the positive things you have going for you in your classroom. Do you have a good view out of your windows? How can you make the best use of it? Do you have interesting wall surfaces? How can you accent them? Are the colors in your room neutral so that you can do interesting things with accent colors? In other words, how can you and your pupils emphasize whatever is potentially good in your room so that its imperfections become less noticeable?

By way of example, let's see what can be done to brighten wall surfaces—a formidable task in many classrooms. Walls can fulfill an important function in classroom or home in that they can be used to mirror our values, and thus serve as a constant reinforcement of what we say and do.

Prepare a wall inventory. How many different wall surface areas do you have? How large are they? How will you affix materials to the various surfaces? Think imaginatively, and then set about to see that your walls communicate your enthusiasm for living and learning—and your pupils' enthusiasm.

If you have a surface area in which you can stick pins, place a box of pins and a box full of bright yarn skeins nearby. Encourage pupils to create abstract line designs with the yarn and pins. If you have an acoustical tile ceiling you can create designs by sticking golf tees in the little holes and winding yarn from tee to tee in interesting patterns. Encourage your pupils to change the designs frequently.

A window is a transparent wall. Paste bits of colored cellophane on the window, and these will create moving colored patterns on pupils, desks, floor, and walls as the sun's rays move during the day. Sheets of bright construction paper affixed here and there on wall surfaces will complement the colored cellophane nicely, and add considerable color to the room.

If your classroom windows contain panes or sections that can be covered with standard sheets of paper (e.g., 12″ × 18″), ask individual pupils to select a pane and reproduce the view they see through it, using whatever art medium strikes their fancy. Then paste those pupils' drawings and paintings in the appropriate window panes, and for several days the class will look out those window panes through Mary's and Jimmy's and Susan's eyes. An automobile, a bird, or an airplane viewed through a pane by the artist is frozen in that space as long as his work of art covers the window pane, which is an interesting idea to muse over with your class. It's also interesting to discover how much the view has changed when you remove the picture and once again look through the pane. Arrange things so that several window panes are always covered this way. It makes a nice effect.

Construct a large flat paper tree on a wall area where you can leave it up all year long. Encourage your pupils to decorate it and the surrounding area in keeping with seasonal changes. As the leaves begin to change color outside, change the color of the leaves on your paper tree. Remove birds as their real counterparts fly south. Add "snow" to the bare branches whenever it snows during the winter. Think of the excitement in your room when a pupil comes to school with the news that he has seen the first robin or the first daffodil. Let pupils add paper flowers and animals as they discover them outside in spring. Leave the paper tree and other forms of life up at the end of the school year as a legacy for your next class, who can then pick up the chain of life where your last class left off.

Move beyond mere walls to the total environment. For example, place several different colored slips of paper in a box and draw one out each Friday just before dismissal. Then see how much of that color you and your pupils can introduce into the classroom during the next week. Suppose you selected blue. Display pictures in which blues dominate. Ask your pupils to feature blues in their art work. Use blues in your bulletin board displays. Display blue book jackets. Try to match the blue of the sky each day. Ask pupils to bring blue objects to school. Pupils will probably wear blue clothes. Line up such pupils in a row beginning with the lightest blue article and continuing to the darkest blue. It's probable that no two will wear the same exact color.

Select a different color each week. Your class will enjoy it, and they'll learn a lot about color variation in the process—and in an interesting and cheerful classroom too!

WORK TOWARD A CLEAN CLASSROOM

Teachers have long been accused—with some justification —of equating neatness with goodness. The neat pupil with his careful handwriting and clean desk seemed to have an edge on his opposite when it came to teacher approval and grades. The result was that somehow cleanliness and neatness came to be scorned by pupils as traits found mainly in sissies and teachers' pets. Far better to be overly untidy than to give the impression that cleanliness was a virtue worth considering. This feeling seems to run so deep that young people have traditionally adopted unkempt clothing and a slovenly appearance when they wish to show their resentment of adult society.

The tragedy of our inability to communicate the intrinsic worth of a clean environment can be seen in our society's willingness to put up with a horribly littered and polluted environment—and manufactured pollution at that—with its no-return bottles, popsicle sticks, cigarette butts, tin cans, and countless varieties of smoke. In a crowded environment, cleanliness isn't related as much to goodness as it almost is to survival, a fact discovered by anyone who moves into a small apartment or house trailer. Our society as a whole still has to learn this lesson, and to see an unpolluted environment in its proper context.

What better place is there to tackle this critical social problem than in the classroom? All the societal elements are there: crowded conditions, lots of activity, waste materials, and great variation in the values and self-discipline of the inhabitants. It's almost a perfect situation in which to explore individual and group behavior and values.

Traditional social studies units on pollution tended to focus on community and regional problems that children should be aware of, but that they have little control over. Since your study will deal primarily with an exploration of pupil values and behavior, focus it on pollution problems that they can actually deal with—and there are plenty of those around any school.

You might begin by looking into the essential nature of dirt, litter, and pollution. At what point does a clean classroom become dirty, littered, or polluted? How clean should a classroom be? Is it worth the effort it takes to keep a classroom that clean? These are difficult questions to explore since opinions will vary greatly. In addition, you'll get pat answers from some pupils and flip answers from others, unless you can clearly indicate in your initiating activity that this study will be an honest and freely conceived exploration into the nature of the environment you all will live in during the school year.

Several investigations will suggest themselves. First, enough differences of opinion will exist to suggest a survey of the opinions your pupils have. Second, it's also obvious that you will have problems with definitions, so your pupils might consult books and authorities. How do Webster and your school custodian define litter? Do the teachers in your school differ in their views as to how clean a classroom should be? A third investigation might be concerned with the amount of dirt and waste that actually exists in your classroom. Your pupils might keep records, weighing waste paper for several weeks. How much was placed in the wastebasket each day and how much was picked off the floor? Can they figure out ways of measuring the amount of dust and dirt on the floor? Does it differ from day to day? Do patterns become evident? How much of the dirt and litter are they responsible for and how much came into the room through other means?

Investigations such as these will soon lead into larger social questions that are well worth discussing with your class:

1. Is there a difference between a person tracking mud into a room that only he uses and into a classroom that thirty pupils share? (Is there a difference between smoking a cigarette alone in a room or in a room that several other people also occupy?) If there is a difference, what is the reason for this difference, and why should or shouldn't the mud tracker (or cigarette smoker) be concerned about the feelings of others? What about factories that employ hundreds of people but whose smokestacks pollute the air? What about cities that dump sewage into rivers that run past downstream cities and towns?

2. Does a person who buys a candy bar have a right to consume only the part he enjoys—the candy—letting someone else (who got no share of the candy) dispose of the wrapper he has thrown to the ground?

3. Should standards of cleanliness vary in different situations?

If so, what criteria should be used? How is health related to cleanliness? How should differences of opinion be resolved?

4. What is the role of the professional clean-up person in our society? Your pupils will discover that exploring this phenomenon can prove most interesting. How much of the advertising space in newspapers, magazines, and on TV is devoted to products and services that help keep ourselves and our environment clean and tidy? How many different occupations can your pupils discover that relate directly or indirectly to this—and how many members of their families are involved in this work (barbers, custodians, vacuum cleaner salesmen, dry cleaners, maids, window washers, painters, etc.)? Invite your school custodian into your room to discuss his work and your pupils' relationship to his work. Even though he is charged with the overall task of keeping the school clean, pupils and teachers still have a primary responsibility to help clean up whatever mess they make.

Given the right kind of classroom group, your discussions and explorations will lead you to the point where your class will want to decide the level of cleanness (or dirtiness) they can comfortably live with in their classroom. Your explorations might involve the class not cleaning your classroom for several days or more to see at what point you as a group become uncomfortable with the way things are. Why did you as a group become uncomfortable? What advantages does a clean room have over a dirty one?

At this point your unit will undoubtedly veer off into problems that our larger society faces. Your pupils should begin to see parallels between the problems you have explored and the problems a city council wrestles with in creating a comfortable environment for the citizens of a city. We must all begin to see individual responsibility as crucial to the solution of such problems. If it's difficult to find a trash can to dispose of a candy bar wrapper, it's also difficult to find ways of disposing the waste materials from a manufacturing plant. But both searches are essential. Cleanliness isn't just a matter of "being good." Rather, it's a matter of facing up to the problems of having to live with each other.

Your study should end with the development of policies

that govern your group's behavior relative to the level of cleanliness sought in your classroom. Your policies will probably be less stringent than some would wish and tighter than others would wish. This is a continuing problem in dealing with environmental controls. Hopefully, your pupils will gain new insights into the problems pollution can raise in a community, and hopefully they will constantly seek ways to make your classroom and school a cleaner, more pleasant place—not because they are sissies or teachers' pets, but because they actually prefer that kind of environment.

THINK BEYOND YOUR CLASSROOM

Odd as it might seem, many pupils who will make a reasonable effort to keep their own classroom clean and attractive will show far less concern for school areas they share with other classes—corridors, restrooms, playground, cafeteria, etc. Don't be unduly surprised at this apparent contradiction. It's a behavioral phenomenon that apartment dwellers, park maintenance people, and others similarly situated understand only too well.

This contradiction defines a major task you face as an elementary teacher in a democratic society—that of developing in your pupils a sense of awareness and concern for democratic institutions in their entirety, and not just only for those small parts that are uniquely theirs. We see abuses at all levels—from the senator whose voting record consistently betrays a narrow range of special interests to the young couple who blithely pick a bouquet of flowers from the display beds in the public park.

The elementary school is ideally organized for an exploration of this problem, so think beyond your classroom and help your pupils discover their proper relationship to the whole school and, by extension, to their entire community, state, region, and country.

Institutions are composed of two parts, an outside surface that is visual evidence of the existence of the institution, and an inside spirit that breathes life into the institution.

The Surface

One interesting way to become acquainted with your school is to explore the multitude of surfaces that cover it. Help your pupils find little niches and corners. Look at weeds that have grown through cracks in the walks. Count the variety of colors, textures, and materials used throughout the building. Make crayon rubbings. Explore the living and non-living ground surfaces. What animal life shares the school building and grounds with the pupils and staff? Where has weathering made subtle changes in interior and exterior coloring? Where have handrails and door handles been rubbed smooth with usage? What walkways have been worn into the schoolyard and floors? Look. Touch. Feel. The surfaces of an institution are dead, but they tell a tale of life. Explore this tale with your pupils and they will begin to see their school in a new light, and view themselves as an integral part of a long parade of pupils and teachers who have come and gone and left their mark.

Move then to an exploration of the pupils' relationship with the school's surfaces that extend beyond their classroom—those parts of a school that often dramatically communicate the prevailing values of the people who live and work there. Begin by focusing on the corridor, restrooms, and play areas your pupils tend to use most, and then look towards such areas as the library, gymnasium, and cafeteria. Try to get your pupils to see such areas as extensions of their own classroom that should be cared for as they would care for their own classroom. (Will your pupils one day see our national parks as extensions of their backyards, downtown sidewalks as extensions of the walks around their homes?)

You might assign a group of pupils to each of these areas. Ask them to study use patterns and to suggest ways in which your class might make these areas more inviting. Don't moralize. Rather, concern yourself with the fascinating challenge of making a corridor or drinking fountain or section of shrubbery more inviting—simply because it will then make life a bit more pleasant.

It's probable that your pupils' first suggestions will relate to clean-up activities—picking up litter, pulling weeds, erasing marks. That's fine, but try to lead them to think beyond mere clean-up activities. Plant bulbs in the fall for spring enjoyment. Set up attractive displays on the corridor walls and bulletin boards. Construct and hang mobiles and wind chimes. Identify and tag trees and shrubs. Encourage your pupils to think imaginatively and to seek interesting and exciting ways of making the surface of school as vibrant as its spirit can and should be.

The Spirit

This chapter began with a discussion of the almost indefinable spirit that permeates every institution. Schools have historically attempted to develop and maintain this abstract spirit and tradition through a variety of concrete rituals and symbols —athletic teams, school songs and chants, school nicknames, school papers, mascots, identifying sweaters, etc. We speak of school loyalty and school spirit. We can sense it in its positive and negative forms quite soon after we enter a school and it becomes more evident the longer we remain.

Explore this elusive phenomenon with your class. How many such rituals and symbols can they identify in your school? How strong are these rituals and symbols in shaping the behavior of teachers and pupils? How necessary are they in developing and maintaining genuine school spirit? What can be done to develop a positive school spirit? What specifically can your class do?

Hard questions with no pat answers. But teachers and pupils can make positive beginnings if they care enough to work at it. Thus, genuine concern for a pleasant living and learning environment will have to begin with you. If you don't have it, you certainly won't be able to develop it in your pupils. If you have it, then you must believe that you can get your pupils to share your concern. Only then will you feel the efforts you will have to expend to be worth the effort.

SIX

Using Imaginative Teaching Methods

to Increase Positive Behavior

*T*oday's TV generation is caught up with discovery. They are as excited about space exploration as children must have been hundreds of years ago when sailing ships opened new worlds. They would rather solve problems than memorize formulas and rules. They want to know what's beneath the surface of things. Unfortunately, they also seem to have little patience with slowly developing skills and understandings that are prerequisites for a trip to the moon. Instant multiplication tables!

The world has unfolded tremendously for them through TV, interstate highways, the paperback revolution, scientific breakthroughs, and other cultural changes. Also, leading scholars in the various disciplines have become interested in the elementary school and in the development of new and challenging curricular materials.

We know that the world will wait for our pupils to grow up even though they don't, but we must still teach imaginatively to encourage and maintain that spirit of excitement and adventure in learning that each generation must develop in the next generation. Good teachers have always known that the quantity of misbehavior in the aisles is directly related to the quality of the teaching in the front of the room, and that boredom needn't be a major problem in classroom life.

Two themes, structure and discovery, seem to permeate the newer elementary school curricular developments. These themes open many exciting possibilities for imaginative teaching that can catch your pupils up in the spirit of learning—and as a bonus, diminish much classroom misbehavior.

Explore these themes with your pupils. Your explorations will modify traditional classroom relationships, and it will force you to change your usual way of doing things—but it can also get your pupils so excited about school that you will face a whole new set of behavior problems, positive problems that arise when pupils work together in the solution of problems they see as very relevant to their needs. Let's take a closer look at these two themes.

INTRODUCE STRUCTURE TO YOUR PUPILS

As an elementary school pupil I memorized several formulas for finding area: S^2 for the area of a square, LW for a rectangle, 1/2BA for a triangle, BA for a parallelogram, $1/2 A[(B_1 + B_2)]$ for a trapezoid and r^2pi for a circle. The formulas had an incomprehensible magical quality about them, and I often confused one for another.

Things cleared up one day about a decade later while I was teaching area to my pupils. In a blazing flash of insight, I suddenly discovered that there is really but one formula for area: the number of square measuring units that fit along the base of an area times the number of such rows that can be

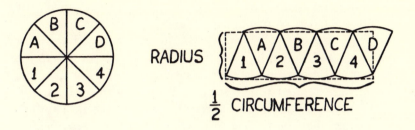

FIGURE 6

placed within the entire area—or length times width as the formula read.

The various formulas did nothing but rearrange or expand the area into a rectangle so that the square measuring units would fit neatly. For example, it's impossible to fit square measuring units into a circle, so the circle is rearranged as illustrated in Figure 6. With a few adjustments here and there, the circle takes on a rectangular shape with a base equal to half the circumference and an altitude equal to the radius. Since the diameter times pi equals the circumference, the radius times pi equals half the circumference. Thus, the area of the "rectangle" formed from the circle is found by multiplying the radius times pi (base) times the radius (altitude). And that's how r^2pi came into being as the formula for the area of a circle. How simple! How pleasant to discover it—albeit a decade late.

It's probable that millions made this discovery before I did, but it was still exciting for me, a young teacher, to discover that all area formulas are related. It added vitality to my teaching of that subject. It was my introduction to the idea of structure, although I didn't realize it at the time.

Although the idea of the structure of a discipline has been around for a long time, Jerome Bruner did much to disseminate the idea among educators through his fascinating little book, *The Process of Education* (Harvard, 1960). In it, Bruner reported for a group of 35 distinguished scholars who met for two weeks in 1959 to explore ways in which science education might be improved. Their conclusions keynoted much of the curricular innovation that occurred during the sixties, and made the concept of structure an important part of such innovation.

The structure of a subject is the set of broad unifying principles and generalizations that tie a subject or discipline together and govern the action of specific examples or phenomena that are related to the subject. It's the answer you might get if you ask a person who is very knowledgeable in a subject to describe what the subject is all about in a few simple words. The relationship of the various formulas for finding area to the single area measurement principle that exists is a simple example of the idea of structure. Newton's third law of motion—for every action there is an equal and opposite reaction—is another. Newton's law can be used to explain the flight of a rocket, the operation of a skateboard, the gyrations of a blown-up and released balloon, and the dunking a person might get when stepping from an unsecured rowboat to the wharf. If a person grasps the structure of a subject, he has learned how to relate it meaningfully to other things.

Bruner argues that every subject has its structure, its own rightness and beauty, and that the underlying simplicity of things evolves out of this structure. Only by learning the structure of a subject can we hope to appreciate its intrinsic meaning.

To those who suggest that the teaching of these fundamental structural principles poses an impossible task to elementary teachers, Bruner and his colleagues reply that, on the contrary, all children can grasp the essence of any subject in some intellectually honest form. What teachers need to do is to think differently about their task, and to approach their pupils in a spirit of exploration.

Many of the curricular materials you are now using are written so that your pupils can discover the structure of the topics they study, and you can expect more of this in the years ahead. You can prepare yourself for more effective teaching with these materials by seeking major unifying principles and generalizations in your teaching, and by exploring them with your pupils. Find relationships between school and community life.

Encourage your pupils to look at things, to handle things, to engage in convergent and divergent modes of dealing with things—to create a storehouse of related mental images of the world about them. Compare and contrast phenomena whenever possible in school activities. Build your units around major principles instead of around merely descriptive terms and categories.

To begin, you might explore the following generalizations with your pupils. They deal with traditional subject areas, and thus they provide plenty of exploratory possibilities on familiar ground. Don't hesitate to rephrase the statements to fit your situation.

Art Is the Celebration of the Ordinary. This fresh interpretation of art by the gifted midwestern artist, Reinhold Marxhausen, is just the sort of generalization that an imaginative teacher and a room full of pupils can explore with abandon.

What Marxhausen suggests is that artists seek beauty in all sorts of ordinary things such as trees, fences, faces, buildings, and shapes—and that they demonstrate their joy at finding beauty by lavishing their time and energy on the object, by celebrating it as it were. They paint it bigger than life. They cast it in bronze. They increase the brilliance of the color. They adjust shapes to make the composition more pleasing. They display it attractively. Think of Van Gogh and a bowl of sunflowers, Durer and two praying hands, Rouault and a clown.

Is Marxhausen correct? Study art objects with your pupils to see what subjects attract the attention of artists. Do artists "celebrate" the ordinary things that we don't often even notice? What about abstract art? What about photography, wallpaper designs, jewelry, architecture? What about pop artists who do oil paintings of soup cans and soap boxes?

Chances are, the more you and your pupils explore Marxhausen's generalization, the more truth you will discover in it, and the deeper will grow your understanding of what an artist does and why he does it. More importantly, these explorations should spark a more meaningful art program in your classroom. Your pupils will open their eyes to the world about them, and they too will begin to "celebrate" those things that interest and

excite them—dandelions, bits of construction paper, Christmas trees, pussy willows, pumpkins.

Arithemetic Is the Seach for a Simpler Way to Communicate Quantity. I could tell you that I am $2 + [2\,(63 \div 3)]$ years old, and it would be correct. You would rather have me express the same quantity in simpler terms—that I am 44 years old. That's the essence of arithmetic, one of the written language arts. By manipulating ten digits and a number of other symbols through standard operations, we can communicate quantity more clearly and efficiently with numerals than we could with spelled-out words.

In working arithmetic problems in their simplest form, a person reduces a collection of quantitative data on one side of an equation to a simple term on the other side. Any such equation can be solved by counting, but it might take awhile. Set manipulations help keep things in focus, and the various processes, properties, and operations speed up the solution of the equation.

One way to explore this with your pupils is to give them a set of three or four multiplication problems such as 23×8. Ask them to work the problems three times: (1) by counting out the answers (count to 23 eight times cumulating the total), (2) by addition (add a column of eight 23's), and (3) by multiplication. Keep a record of the time it takes each pupil to work the problems through each method. Compute the average times for the class for each method, and compare results. Multiplication should come in first and addition second every time.

Through activities such as this you can help your pupils discover that the multiplication tables are a means to an end and not an end in themselves; that the commutative property eliminates the need to learn many of the multiplication facts as separate and distinct facts; that accuracy, clarity, and efficiency are as important in arithmetic as they are in speaking and writing. You can help your pupils discover these and other things if you will make the idea of an equation the center of every arithmetic lesson you teach—because in the final analysis, all arithmetic activity is grounded in the equation.

Song Is the Slowing Down of Speech in Order to Savor Nuance. Marshall McLuhan's intriguing generalization can put a lot more meaning and enjoyment into your music program.

It takes ten seconds to speak the 38 word text of Handel's "Hallelujah Chorus," and it takes four minutes to sing it—but what a difference! When we speak, we usually talk in an evenly modulated voice and let our choice of words carry the emotional message we wish to communicate. By slowing down our speech and by repeating words or phrases as we sing, we have many opportunities to use the elements of music (tone, melody, rhythm, volume, and form) to communicate emotions. When we sing we don't need to use nearly as many adjectives and adverbs, because our voice modulations take care of those aspects of communication.

Explore this fascinating phenomenon with your pupils. Can they discover relationships between solo and group singing, between unison and part singing? What can they discover about categories of songs—the blues, hymns, folk songs, lullabies, patriotic songs? Why can we place such songs in categories? What relationships exist between the melodic and rhythmic capabilities of the human voice and the musical instruments we use to supplement our voices? What human limitations exist in communicating through song, and how have the newer developments in electronics and recording stretched those capabilities?

Don't hesitate to draw on the records young people listen to today. These recording groups are the troubadours and barber shop quartets of today. Their music may sound disjointed to you at first hearing, but it is often as intricate as a finely woven Bach fugue—and it does communicate to children who are being reared in an electronic age.

Once you see singing as a means of introducing emotions into speech by slowing it down, your entire music program will take on a new meaning. You will then not teach the elements of music as ends in themselves, but rather as exciting tools that permit your pupils to make the most of their communicative potential. "Imagine! This year in music lessons we're going to learn how to say more by talking slowly!"

Work towards the day when you can say things like this to your pupils, "This was really a wonderful experience we had on our field trip. Normally, we would write a story about it, but I can see that you're all so excited about what we did that words alone won't do the job. The only way we can say how we feel is by creating songs about our experience and singing them."

Well, why not?

Below are some additional generalizations that you and your pupils might explore. Each has the potential to open up a whole new world of exciting meaning in your teaching; and each can help you and your pupils discover other and perhaps even more interesting generalizations about a variety of subjects that lead to a better understanding and appreciation of man's knowledge and the nature of the school in our society.

> Geography is the study of where things are and why they are there.
>
> Literature is an interpretation of reality.
>
> Science is the study of the interaction of matter and energy, and the changes that result from this interaction.
>
> History is a way of looking forward through a mirror.
>
> Recess is a study period.

DISCOVER DISCOVERY WITH YOUR PUPILS

One day when I was in the third grade I was about my business of mastering the nine-times table. I had written the products in a column, and suddenly I noticed an interesting set of patterns. I rushed to my teacher with the information, "The one's column has all the numbers in a row from nine to zero and the ten's column has just the reverse; and when you add the digits of the products you always get the number nine."

My teacher paused, looked down upon me, and replied, "Who doesn't know that?"

Well I didn't, for one. Crestfallen at the obvious insignificance of my discovery, I returned to my seat and continued my memorizations.

9
18
27
36
45
54
63
72
81
90

I began my teaching career in a one room school, and by the second week I had run out of ideas to keep my pupils interested. Casting about desperately for ideas one day, I dredged up my third grade nine-times discovery and introduced it to my pupils. They were much more impressed than my third grade teacher had been. "Do the other multiplication tables do things like that?" one of my pupils asked.

Do they indeed? I had never even thought of going on to the other tables, so great had been my third grade rebuff. But now, with an enthusiastic group of pupils (and with nothing more educationally promising on the immediate horizon), I began to look at the other tables. We wrote them all in columns and added the digits. Then we looked at what we found and became increasingly excited about our discoveries. For example, the eight-times table looked like this:

sums of the digits
of the products

8 — 8
16— 7
24— 6
32— 5
40— 4
48—12—3
56—11—2
64—10—1
72— 9
80— 8
88—16—7
96—15—6

That's about all we did for several days, and we discovered many fascinating relationships. We found that certain tables were similar to others. When we looked at the sequence of digits in the one's column (e.g., 8, 6, 4, 2, 0, etc., in the eights), the one and nine, two and eight, three and seven, and four and six times tables were similar, but reversed, and these pairs of numbers always added up to ten.

When we examined the sums of the digits of the various tables, the one and eight, two and seven, three and six, and four and five times tables were similar, but reversed, and these pairs of numbers always added up to nine. How odd. We puzzled over what the sums of the digits implied, and through this exploration we finally discovered what casting-out-nines was really all about.

We wrote the numerals from zero to ninety-nine in 10×10 tables and drew circles around the products of the various multiplication tables. We discovered interesting visual patterns and discovered that certain tables were related to others visually. The seven-times table is illustrated below:

```
 ⓪  1  2  3   4   5  6 ⑦  8  9
10 11 12 13 ⑭ 15 16 17 18 19
20 ㉑ 22 23 24 25 26 27 ㉘ 29
30 31 32 33 34 ㉟ 36 37 38 39
40 41 ㊷ 43 44 45 46 47 48 ㊾
50 51 52 53 54 55 ㊱ 57 58 59
60 61 62 ㊳ 64 65 66 67 68 69
㊀ 71 72 73 74 75 76 ㊐ 78 79
80 81 82 83 ㊳ 85 86 87 88 89
90 ㊛ 92 93 94 95 96 97 ㊾ 99
```

We made many other discoveries and it was a truly exciting experience because we were all exploring together in an atmosphere free from traditional school time, space, grade patterns, and procedures.

And then about eight years later I ran across Irving Adler's book, *Magic House of Numbers* (Signet, 1957), and discovered that many of our discoveries had already been discovered and were in print. It was of little concern. Adler (or someone else) may have discovered them, but we did too—and no one could take our discoveries away from us this time.

More importantly, the experience taught me how exciting school can be when a teacher and his pupils discover things together. Discovery teaching has been around for a long time in a variety of forms and under a variety of names. Call it what you will; it is essentially an approach to teaching that emphasizes the *processes* a person uses to explore phenomena. Problems are often drawn from the immediate environment and are narrowed until they can be solved by the class. Answers are not known in advance. Indeed, the teacher deliberately withholds information until the pupils themselves discover a need for it. Pupils take the lead in proposing hypotheses and ways of gathering and manipulating data in the solution of the problem. Activities are *why* centered—"How do we know?" "Why did it turn out this way?" "How can we make sure?" etc. The teacher's major tasks are to expedite discovery by providing needed materials and to answer questions pupils would be unable to answer on their own.

Educators suggest that this kind of intellectual activity is especially important today because man's knowledge has increased at such a rapid rate that it is better to concentrate our energies on teaching children how to seek answers to problems than it is to try to pump them full of answers. My pupils and I learned something important about the multiplication tables through our explorations, but the exploration itself was at least as important in the long run. I also discovered that during our explorations the boredom I had been so concerned about disappeared and was replaced with genuine enthusiasm for learning. It was a significant discovery for a young teacher to make.

The A.A.A.S. elementary science program, Science: A Process Approach, has identified fourteen processes that a person uses to solve problems. These form the core of discovery teaching programs. Five are especially suited to beginning explorations in your immediate classroom environment: observing, inferring, measuring, classifying, and predicting. Work first with these. Start with the suggestions that follow or with variations of your own. Observe your pupils' reactions to the activities. What changes in behavior do you see? How will you deal with these changes? What adjustments will you have to make in your teaching if you adopt curricular programs oriented around discovery processes such as these? How can you modify your teaching to emphasize discovery procedures?

Observing

Any investigation of an object begins with those characteristics that are directly perceived by the senses. The investigator observes with all appropriate sense organs so that he can describe the object as accurately as possible.

A Left-Hand Laboratory. It isn't necessary to have a lot of equipment to explore the nature of observation. You can begin with your pupils' left hands.

Divide your class into groups of four or five pupils. Ask each pupil to examine his left hand intently for several minutes, and then to write in precise terms all the observations he can make of it.

Caution pupils to write only things that they can observe directly, and not interpretations they might make on the basis of their observations (inferences). For example, some pupils might *observe* long blue lines or ridges under the skin on the top side of their hand, but they only *infer* (and not observe) that these are veins.

Pupils should look for properties and conditions. A property is a trait or attribute of an object—the covering on my hand is flexible; the surface on my fingernails is smooth. A condition is a state of being—my hands are dirty; my fingernails have been cut recently.

Encourage them to ask questions such as: How many? How large? How long? What similarities and differences exist? Observation uses all senses, so they should smell, taste, feel, shake, and listen, as well as look when they gather information on their hands. How might such tools as rulers, pins, graph paper, calipers, and lengths of string help them make more accurate observations?

Perhaps some pupils will want to make their observations blindfolded, or with their left hand in a glove or sack, or with their hand immersed in water.

After each pupil has written several observations, ask the members of each group to compare and discuss their lists, and to change or eliminate inaccurate observations. Were any observations made by everyone in the group? Were any observations true of only one person in the group?

Then bring all the groups together and discuss the observations the class made. It's probable that only two or three identical observations will have been made by every pupil in the class. Place the left hands of several pupils right next to each other to note the variation that exists. Arrange hands from shortest to longest, from darkest to lightest color, from smoothest to roughest skin.

No doubt about it, your pupils will treat their left hands with new respect from now on—and yours too—especially if you just happened to show up in school that day with a diamond ring weighing down your left hand!

Manufactured Variation. Most people think that standardized manufactured items are identical. Careful observation will show differences, however.

Gather a dozen or so examples of each of several sets of such machine-made objects as Ping-Pong balls, paper clips, plastic spoons, pencils, etc. Divide your class into groups and give each group a different set of objects. Ask them to discover differences in their set of objects.

At first they won't be able to find differences, but it won't be long before they will figure out ways to discover the slight variations in weight, length, and color that exist. They will find nicks and cracks, marks and smudges—especially if they have access to a magnifying glass. Challenge them to discover a unique observation in each object in their collection of similar items.

After this experience, your pupils should be able to discover many differences in sets of such "non-manufactured" items as maple leaves, pine cones, flowers, twigs, apples, and carrots.

What 18 Hours Can Do. To help your pupils become more aware of their classroom surroundings, ask them to make observations of their classroom the last thing one afternoon and the first thing the next morning, and to note any changes that occurred overnight.

Shadows will have changed; a flower might have opened; the wastebasket will have been emptied; an open window might be closed; the temperature might have changed.

Go one step further. Give each pupil a special spot: a patch of floor, a chalkboard, a window pane, a desk top, a bulletin board. Ask pupils to observe changes that occurred overnight in their spaces.

Make changes in the room after pupils leave each day. Are they able to spot the changes the next morning? Do they get better as time goes on, especially in spotting the less obvious changes? (One teacher removed the flag. The next morning her class went through the entire Pledge of Allegiance and no one noticed the flag was missing. Needless to say, that teacher set up all sorts of activities to help her pupils become more aware of their surroundings.)

Note the clothes your pupils wear from day to day. What differences can they observe on successive days? What effect does the weather have on clothes selection? What colors seem to dominate? Bring newspaper ads featuring children's clothing. Can your pupils match their clothes with clothing pictured in the ads?

Observation Objects. Many common objects lend themselves well to imaginative observation activities. Start with these and see where they will take you: a square of wax paper with a water drop on it; little piles of Jell-O powder, Kool-Aid, chili powder, cornmeal, etc,; a potato chip or a cornflake; a little square of elm leaf or crepe paper; a piece of tapioca or a grain of rice.

Observe objects that will change during the observation period: an ice cube; a burning candle; a cube of Jell-O; a sugar cube dropped in water; an ink drop dropped into a glass of cool water, and another drop dropped into a glass of warm water.

And, of course, the most changeable set of observations your pupils can make is to make one observation of you and your behavior every fifteen minutes during the school day. Won't their lists make interesting reading after school? Will you be able to differentiate the observations from the inferences?

Inferring

Inferences are statements about objects or events that are based on observations, but that are not the result of direct perception. An inference is an explanation of an observation that comes from thinking about the observation, and that usually draws heavily on past experiences that were somewhat similar. Inferences play an important part in our lives, so they're well worth exploring with your pupils.

"I Make Inferences for a Living." Begin by exploring occupations that draw heavily on inferences. The medical doctor is perhaps the most familiar illustration to use with your pupils. He listens to the symptoms his patients describe, examines their skin, checks their blood pressure, listens to their heart, taps their chest, makes laboratory tests, etc. On the basis of all these observations and his previous experience with similar observations, he makes a diagnosis and prescribes a remedy. His success, to an extent, is based on his ability to use inferences to make accurate diagnoses.

Ask your pupils to describe inferences that their parents make in their work. Perhaps there is a geologist in the group— or a plumber, a mechanic, a stock broker, a newspaper reporter, a salesman, a farmer, a taxicab driver, a waitress, a nurse, a secretary, a department store buyer. All these occupations and many others require careful observations and intelligent inferences for success. Can your pupils suggest what observations and inferences are required in the occupations listed above? In their parents' occupations? Your discussion might start slowly, but it should become exciting once your pupils grasp that inferential decisions form the foundation of most occupations.

Ask your pupils to indicate observations and inferences you make in your work as a teacher. You might get them started by mentioning that you observe the weather, and infer whether or not outdoor play is advisable; you observe their reactions to a lesson and infer whether you should continue according to plan or make changes; you observe a pupil's behavior and infer whether or not he is sick. Let your pupils suggest other observations and inferences you make during the day.

Do your pupils make inferences during the day? Use these for starters and let them add others: Do their stomachs tell them that the hands of the clock must be nearing noon? Does the current class activity tell them that the school day is almost over? Does a film can on your desk in the morning tell anything about what might happen later in the day? Does a new bulletin board display signal a new science unit?

The Black Box. Variations on the Black Box can provide many fascinating inference activities. The Black Box is, essentially, little more than a closed box or sack with something inside. The pupils may explore it only on the outside. They can shake it, smell it, poke it—do anything to it but open it—and thus try to discover what is inside.

Construct a Black Sack. Place a couple of marbles and Ping-Pong balls and some aromatic spice inside a balloon. Partially blow up the balloon and insert the balloon inside a small grocery sack so it's sort of loose. Can your pupils infer what objects are inside the sack? Make several identical Black Sacks and let a small group work with each one.

When all inferences have been made, discuss their findings with them—but don't tell them what is really inside, even if all pupils agree in their findings. This activity can help pupils understand that scientists frequently have to work at levels in which they do not know for absolutely sure whether or not their inferences are correct.

Construct a Black Box from an ordinary shoe box. Glue several small wooden blocks together on the inside base of the box so that they make a structure of sorts. Tape the top of the box to the box, and make a series of closely spaced pin holes all over the top. Then give your pupils a short length of wire and see if they can figure out the shape of the wooden structure by probing the interior of the box through the pin holes, and by measuring distances.

Several of your pupils will certainly want to create Black Boxes of their own that require others to determine the kind and amount of objects inside, the arrangement of a maze a marble runs through, the operation of a device or simple motor inside, or something else. You'll be surprised at the elaborate constructions they'll make.

Odd Packages. Blow up an empty candy bar wrapper and place it on a plate with several full candy bars. Ask your pupils to devise ways of discovering the empty wrapper without touching it.

Switch the contents of several popular cereal boxes and ask your pupils if they can match the proper contents with the proper boxes. They might be able to differentiate by smell or by a characteristic sound certain cereals have when shaken. They might also note the weights on the boxes and weigh the boxes. They might suggest other observations on which to base their inferences, perhaps just feeling inside.

Taped Sounds. Ask a group of pupils to use the tape recorder to record a variety of sounds around the school. Then replay the tape for your class to see if your pupils can infer where various segments were taped: the lunch room, the office, the heating plant, the playground, the nurse's office, etc.

You might tape the voices of your pupils' parents at a PTA function. Ask them to refrain from identifying themselves by name during their statement, but to give a clue or two. Can your pupils identify their own and their classmates' parents by the sound of their voices and by the clues they gave?

Isolate common sounds and tape them out of their normal

context: the sounds of a pencil sharpener, water faucet, type-writer, bouncing ball, door slamming. Can your pupils identify the sounds?

Tape short segments of popular TV shows and replay them for your class. Erase words and names that will easily identify the shows. What observations can your pupils make that will help them make inferences about what kind of a show it is, the audience it might be directed to, the time of day it might be on, and its identity?

Measuring

If you asked your pupils to collect some measurement data on the shrubs in your schoolyard, they would probably respond initially in two ways: they would count the shrubs, and they would measure their heights. This response underscores a very curious phenomenon about measurement, something worth exploring with your pupils.

The first response, to count the shrubs, makes use of an inexact unit of measurement, *the shrub,* but it results in an exact count of the number of shrubs in the yard. The shrub is an inexact measuring tool because each shrub is different from all other shrubs—in size, shape, age, weight, etc.—and yet each is counted a shrub. There are no half shrubs.

The second response, to measure the height of the shrubs, draws on *the ruler,* one of a number of very exact measuring tools our society has developed. Yet, the results will be anything but exact. Ten measurings of the height of a shrub will result in ten different measurements, with a probable variation of several inches between the shortest and longest measurements.

Thus, when we measure we use discrete and continuous measuring tools. Discrete tools are counting tools, inexact in the structure of their measuring unit but exact in the measurement (count) they give. Continuous measuring tools are exact in that the measuring units are standardized and capable of subdivision for greater accuracy, but they frequently result in inexact measurement due to human error.

The term, *exact,* has been used in the discussion above. As you explore measurement with your pupils, introduce them to the more specific terms, *precision* and *accuracy. Precision* refers to the amount of agreement found in repeated measurements—twelve shrubs every time you count them, but a variation of several inches in ten measurements made of the height of one of the shrubs. *Accuracy* refers to the standardized nature of the measuring tools—shrubs being an inaccurate standard, and inches being quite standard.

Explore these two forms of measurement with your pupils. It will help them develop a better understanding of the significance of measurement in their lives.

Discrete Measurement. Ask your pupils to look for examples of objects that we place under one class even though they may vary much in size, shape, weight, age, etc. Trees, buildings, houses, mountains, cities, and rivers are examples of such things. Then ask them to suggest objects that vary relatively little, that are more standardized. Pencils, eating spoons, marbles, baseball bats, and handkerchiefs are examples of these.

Can your pupils suggest things that are difficult to count? While it's easy to count individual trees, it's more difficult to count forests since it's often hard to tell where one forest ends and another begins. Similarly, it's often difficult to count neighborhoods, deserts, oceans, family relationships, and cold spells.

Some things we count have unusual properties. Highways are only a few feet wide but hundreds of miles long. Fossils may be very small but very old while a skyscraper might be very large but brand new. How do you count Jell-O?

Can your pupils think of new ways of measuring by counting? Can they measure the length of a city block by counting the expansion cracks placed in the sidewalk? Can they measure the size of a school staff by counting the cars in the parking lot? Can they measure the area of the classroom floor and ceiling by counting the tiles? Will the totals be the same? Are the areas the same? Can you tell how cold it is outside on different days by counting the number of jackets in the cloakroom?

Continuous Measurement. Science and mathematics textbooks generally do an adequate job of introducing pupils to the basic measurement tools we use. Your task as teacher is to show your pupils how to explore with these tools.

Introduce your pupils to the need for accurate and objective measurement that doesn't rely entirely on man's sense organs by placing four pans of water on a table. Put ice water and hot water in the two outside pans and lukewarm water (same temperature) in the two inside pans. Ask pupils to place their right and left hands in the outside pans for about a minute, and then to place their hands in the two inside pans. Which of the inside pans is the warmer? Reverse the pans and ask them to try again.

Place five objects on a table. One should be quite heavy and the other quite light. The other three should be between the extremes in weight, and but a few ounces different from each other. Ask pupils to arrange the five objects in order. Note the differences among pupils as they arrange them.

Create your own measuring units: squares of paper for measuring area, marbles for measuring weight, pencils for measuring length. Give names to your measuring units. Ask one group of pupils to measure objects in your classroom using your measuring tools and another group to measure the same objects using standard measuring tools. Compare results. Which group was able to get a more accurate measurement? What problems would arise if everyone used his own measurement system?

Don't overlook the many explorations your pupils can make with the unusual measuring devices available in your classroom: the timer in a tape recorder, the movement of shadows across the classroom, the length of time it takes a pupil to read ten words (or 100 words, etc.), the revolutions a phonograph turntable makes, the weight of any book (textbooks, encyclopedias) of which your room has multiple copies, the amount of warm air arising from the register.

Most science books and materials that deal in any way with measurement give directions for making simple classroom measuring devices. The soda straw balance, the rubber band spring scale, the soda straw hydrometer, and the bubble timer are some common examples. Search these out and encourage your pupils to make them and explore with them. How can you weigh a blade of grass? How can you measure the area of a leaf? How can you tell if milk is denser than orange juice? How much paper is in a paper cup?

An impossible task for children? Not at all if you and they inject a little imagination into the challenge. Who knows— they might even figure out a way to measure how much they learned today!

Classifying

We spend much of our time classifying the world. Pupils learn all sorts of classification schemes in school—from alphabetizing to learning the names of various plants and animals. They compare terms like big and little, and they test tastes like sweet and sour. In a surprisingly short time children master such complex tasks as finding a specific house among the hundreds in their neighborhood. They can master such tasks because the classification schemes we use (such as street and house numbering systems) are often relatively simple even though they encompass large numbers of cases.

In addition to learning specific classification schemes commonly used in our culture, children also need to explore the basic nature of classification. They need to see that classification is essentially a useful though sometimes arbitrary means of grouping objects for easier identification. Objects are usually classified on the basis of observable properties and conditions.

Ignore Traditional Categories. One way to emphasize the important point that any given set of objects can be classified in a number of ways is to re-classify a page from the telephone book. The telephone people classify people alphabetically, and it seems to work quite well. All the more reason your pupils might leap to the challenge of discovering other systems.

Select a page from the book and transfer it to an overhead

transparency (or you might be able to get a dozen or so copies of last year's book from the phone company). Your pupils' first task will be to create the first stage of your classification system—to divide all the names into two (or more) subsets on the basis of an observable property.

What possibilities exist? Literally dozens. People living east and people living west (or north and south) of some major street in town, all people in each of the telephone exchanges used in your area, residences and businesses, phones owned by men and phones owned by women.

But why use such obvious classification schemes? Classify people by the number of letters in their last name, by the sum of the digits in their address, by the national origin of their names, by whether the last letter in their name came in the first or second half of the alphabet.

Once your pupils get into the spirit of the task, they will rise to the challenge of discovering further divisions that will finally reduce each name on the page to a set of which it is the only member.

Discuss the systems your pupils develop and compare them with the system used in the phone book. What advantages and disadvantages are evident in each? (Don't think that an alphabetical classification is without its problems. Have you ever known an address but not the name, the first name but not the last?) Your pupils should discover that a classification scheme will remain in common use only if it is the most useful scheme that people can devise.

Further Explorations. Try the activities suggested below. Each will help you and your pupils discover a bit more about classification, and each should suggest further explorations you might make.

Ask your pupils to classify the words in the week's spelling list. For example, words might be grouped into various classification stages by whether or not they contain double letters (moon, bubble, etc.), by the number of vowels they have, by the number of little words that can be made out of the spelling word, etc. When your pupils have completed their schemes, ask them to explain their schemes to each other. They will be surprised at the variety of criteria they used to group the same set of words.

Place a different object in each of a dozen sacks. Ask pupils to place a hand in each sack and then to classify the twelve objects by feel alone, continuing to group the items until each one is in a class by itself. Compare classification schemes the pupils devise.

Classify the articles on the front page of your local paper using various criteria: good and bad news; local, national, and international news; the number of names used in an article; whether or not the article is continued on another page; headline size, etc. After you've developed a scheme that classifies each article in a separate class, see if you can use the same scheme on front page stories on succeeding days.

Bring a sack of unshelled peanuts to class. Can a group of pupils classify the entire sack so that each peanut ends up in a separate class? Initial categories will probably be based on the number of peanuts in the shell, whether or not the shell has a crack in it, color variations, and other more obvious aspects. In time, though, the group will be challenged to discover more and more sophisticated measuring tools: soda straw balances, holes in cards to measure diameter, water displacement measurements, etc. It's quite a challenge, but it can be done.

Ask each pupil to select an animal, but not to divulge it. Select one pupil as "it." Then announce various categories and ask pupils who fit the category to stand in a stated spot. All pupils who are not in the "it" category are out of the game. Follow "it" from category to category until someone guesses what animal he is. For example, a sequence of categories "it" is in might be: zoo animal/four legs/has spots on body/long neck. By this time someone will guess giraffe.

Call four pupils to the front of the room. Say, "I called these pupils to the front of the room because they all have something in common that you can see. What is it?" Your pupils

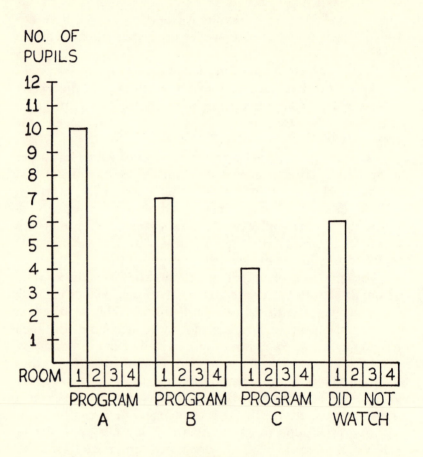

FIGURE 7

might note several properties or conditions common to all:
blond hair, brown shoes, two ears, etc. Can they suggest a
unique factor for each person?

How many different ways can your pupils think of to classify all the pupils in your room so that each is in a unique
class? Can they classify all the arithmetic books so each is in a
separate class? How would they classify all the desks in the room?
What about their hats and caps? Their hair? Their families?

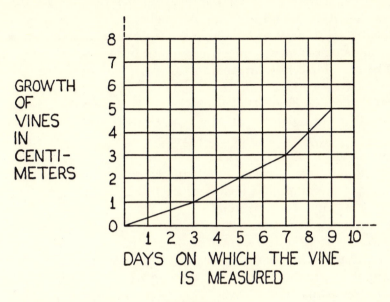

FIGURE 8

Predicting

Much that we do in life is based on predictions: weather reports, business indexes, the time we leave for work in the morning, the scheduling of buses in a transit line, party plans, and weekly grocery shopping.

We are able to predict things because many phenomena occur in regular patterns, and these can be charted or graphed so that predictions can be made on the basis of the data collected.

Scientists consider a prediction to be a special kind of inference based on interpolations or extrapolations from tables or graphs. Scientific investigations are highly predictive. Scientific theories are validated on their ability to predict behavior.

Poll Taking. You might introduce your pupils to prediction by taking a poll of their television viewing habits. Most pupils have heard of TV ratings, and their viewing habits offer many opportunities to explore predictive behavior.

Begin by asking your pupils to list the TV program they watched during a certain time slot the previous evening. Select a time slot that has several popular programs if possible. Graph their responses on a simple bar graph or histogram as shown in Figure 7. Identify your room as Room 1.

Then send a committee of pupils to another room, preferably the same grade level, to ask what programs those pupils watched during that time slot. Graph their responses in the spaces indicated for Room 2. Examine the responses from the two rooms to see if any viewing pattern is suggested, and then try to predict the response you will get from a third classroom. Take such variable factors as grade level, sex division of the class, etc., into consideration.

Graph the responses you get, and see if your class can now make an even more accurate prediction of the viewing habits of a fourth classroom. You might do other rooms, or poll the school staff and compare their viewing habits with the pupils' viewing habits.

Repeat the poll a week later, only this time ask your pupils to predict viewing behavior on the basis of last week's experience. Your pupils may want to carry out this activity for several weeks, checking other time slots, and comparing their viewing habits with the results of national TV rating polls.

Extrapolation. As you collect data and graph it, you may want to make predictions that extend the graph line beyond the observations you have made and graphed. This is called extrapolation.

One interesting way to do this is to graph the growth of a plant. Plant a vine and systematically remove any lateral buds so that the plant's terminal growth can be more easily measured. Attach the vine to a meterstick, taping the vine to the stick as it grows. Graph the growth on a line graph as shown in Figure 8.

After your pupils have made several entries, ask them to make predictions on future growth. Where will the terminal bud be tomorrow? A week from today? On Billy's birthday?

Vary the conditions to see what effect it has on your pupils'

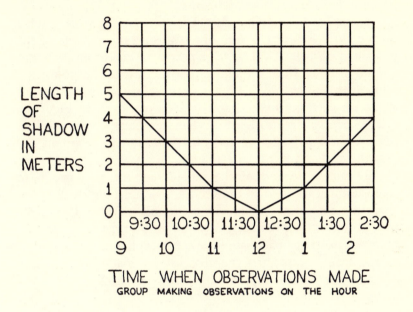

TIME WHEN OBSERVATIONS MADE
GROUP MAKING OBSERVATIONS ON THE HOUR

FIGURE 9

ability to predict growth. For example, quit removing the lateral growth; fertilize heavily; move the plant to a shady spot.

One interesting variation on this activity lasts the entire school year. On the first day of school plant a vine in a large pot placed next to the classroom door. Remove lateral buds to encourage terminal bud growth. Train the vine up the wall several feet, and then start it around the room. The objective of this project is to see if you and your pupils can get the vine to grow completely around the room during the school year, reaching the other side of the classroom door during the last few days of the school year. It's quite a challenge. Pupils will have to chart the growth and predict future growth. If current growth is too slow, they'll have to find out how to encourage growth. If it looks as if the vine is growing too fast, they'll have to find out how to slow down the growth. This project becomes quite exciting by the time spring comes around if it looks as if the vine might make it on schedule.

Interpolation. Divide the class into two groups. Find a spot on the schoolyard where observations can be made of the movement of a shadow cast by a post. Ask one group to measure the distance from the end of the shadow to the post every hour on the hour, and the other group every hour on the half hour. Ask each group to graph its data as shown in Figure 9, but to keep its data to itself. (When complete, the graph line will be U-shaped because the observations will begin in the morning and end in the afternoon.)

Towards the end of the school day ask each group to examine its graph and to determine how long the shadow was when the other group made its measurements. When they make such predictions—predicting a point on a graph between two observations they made—they are interpolating. When both groups have interpolated the observations made by the other group, ask them to compare their graphs to check the accuracy of their observations.

And when they have completed this, you can predict that several pupils will remind you that school should have been out twenty minutes ago.

But that's another problem!

SEVEN

Understanding the Hidden

Causes of Misbehavior

Chapters One through Six suggested that the quantity of misbehavior in the aisles is generally related to the quality of instruction in the front of the room—and that the best way to deal with misbehavior is to so involve pupils in the learning activities you plan for them that misbehavior just doesn't occur. This is certainly the best way to handle misbehavior, but it also presupposes a somewhat unrealistic goal.

Misbehavior will occur in your classroom. There's no escaping it. Your pupils will misbehave and you will deal with them—and you will misbehave and your pupils will deal with you. It's a fact of classroom life. Classroom conditions, various school pressures, personal problems, and differing goals all can lead to the major and minor flare-ups that disrupt the continuity of the planned program.

Since you and your pupils will live with each other's misbehavior, you both should understand the nature of misbehavior and what happens when misbehavior occurs. This chapter will deal with the nature and causes of misbehavior, and the next chapter will deal with the treatment of misbehavior.

EXAMINE THE PRESSURES OF SCHOOL LIFE

Our behavior arises out of a multitude of intrinsic and extrinsic motivations and pressures that shape our behavior and influence our actions—and that generally lead us to behave about as well as we are required to behave. Some of the pressures that affect school behavior are shared by both teachers and pupils, and some are unique to one or the other group. You and your pupils should examine the tensions and pressures of school life and seek ways of living and working together harmoniously despite adverse conditions that might exist.

Pressures Common to Teachers and Pupils

Teachers and pupils share the same school space, and many behavior problems arise because of this. Consider the effect such factors as temperature, humidity, and ventilation can have on a group of people who share a room all day long. The room may be cold in the morning, causing one kind of problem, and smelly and stuffy in the afternoon, causing another kind of problem. Both teachers and pupils may find it difficult to carry on normal classroom activities under such conditions, with smaller irritations rapidly leading to complaining, scolding, name-calling, and other forms of misbehavior in which people in the room are blamed for conditions over which they may actually have no control.

Several other all too common situations also affect both teachers and pupils, creating tensions and pressures that can lead to misbehavior. Crowded conditions, poor lighting, poor acoustics, inappropriate and uncomfortable furniture, noise from outside the classroom, and malfunctioning equipment are among these. Consider, for example, the irritation a flickering fluorescent light or even a poor grade of chalk can cause over a short period of time.

Your class might experiment with an irritating or pressure-laden situation you set up yourself to study your reactions to such situations. One thing that is somewhat simple to do is to systematically reduce the size of your classroom with dividers (or even chalk lines) and note changes in behavior. Continue to reduce the room size a bit more each day until you discover the point at which the pressures of proximity lead to increased behavior problems. What kinds of problems arise? Where do they arise? What time of the day do they arise? Use the answers you get from questions such as these to explore and discuss the effects of other common pressures you and your class face.

One benefit from such study and discussion is that both you and your pupils should become increasingly understanding and tolerant of each other, especially in those situations in which a common problem causes different reactions in different people. For example, a pupil sitting on the outer edge of the class group might not be bothered by crowded conditions as much as a classmate whose desk is located right in the middle of the room, or as another pupil whose desk is located at a spot where there is much room traffic.

Another benefit that can come out of a study of common problem situations is that the group may draw closer together because of the common problem. The best way to begin to deal with a common problem is to admit you have a problem. If the classroom is cold some morning, admit it and adjust your activities accordingly. Let your pupils keep their coats on. Do things that require movement. Huddle together for a story period. You might even go outside for a few minutes and then come back in—the classroom will seem warmer than it seemed before you went out. Sing a few songs. Go to the library. Do things as a group. Through such cohesive activity, smaller disintegrative irritations that could arise out of the situation will be seen in their proper context—as being outside the group—and they will not cause the major disruptions that might otherwise occur.

Pressures That Affect Pupils

Four kinds of pressures commonly affect pupils' behavior: (1) physical and emotional problems, (2) parental expectations, (3) peer acceptance pressures, and (4) instructional and teacher-related pressures.

A number of *physical and emotional problems* can cause pressures that will adversely affect pupils' behavior. Pupils may come to school sick or on the verge of sickness. Family squabbles can leave a pupil tired and emotionally drained. Family financial problems or parental indifference can cause children to come to school hungry. Most pupils are embarrassed when scandal hits their family—an arrest or conviction, parental desertion. Some pupils are embarrassed when their parents require them to wear clothes that don't fit current styles. Bullies can frighten pupils on their way to and from school. The divorce sequence almost always causes anxiety in children.

Some of the above situations will not cause pressures and anxieties in every instance. For example, trouble with the police can be a mark of distinction in some circles, and a marriage break-up a relief in others. Still, situations such as those described above generally do cause pressures that result in distinctive forms of withdrawing behavior—refusing to participate in class activities, sleeping, mumbling, silence. Pupils who have these problems can be easily irritated, and they will flare up briefly and heatedly over real and imagined slights. Even though these problems did not arise in school and cannot be resolved by adjusting school activities, you should still do all you can to relieve the pupils' anxiety by working with the pupil's parents to resolve the problem, and by reducing any side effects that might arise because of school expectations and activities.

Unrealistic parental expectations can be another cause of anxiety in pupils. Pity the average pupil whose "brilliant and talented" brothers and sisters preceded him. Pity the pupil whose parents still keep and display their own straight A elementary school report cards. Pity the pupil whose mother is overly active in organizations that also involve other mothers of school age children. Pity the pupil whose father already plans to "take him into the business." Pity the pupil who gets a dollar for every A he brings home on his report card. Yes, and pity the pupil's teacher in these situations too.

Unrealistic parental expectations can cause much anxiety in teachers as well as in pupils. The teacher often feels constrained to give false reports of good things to help the pupil maintain good relations with his parents, knowing full well that such reports can often come back to haunt him the following year. Pupils beset by unrealistic expectations often resort to fawning kinds of behavior to secure good grades, and sensitive teachers hate to see this sort of self-demeaning behavior in a child. Some pupils bow to the pressures and turn into little grinds, shutting themselves off from much of the informal banter of classroom life in order to score high. Others give up and rebel, refusing to do anything, turning in blank sheets of paper, deliberately doing poor work.

One ray of hope teachers have in dealing with the difficult problem of unrealistic expectations is that such parents are generally willing (even eager) to come to school for conferences. It is probably only in such face-to-face interaction that expectations can be adjusted to realistic levels, and that you can make a strong plea for accepting the child as he is. And then you will probably always want to find activities in which the pupil can achieve success—to reassure his parents and thus reduce the pressure.

Most pupils want to be accepted and liked by their classmates. The insecure worry that they aren't. They worry about their success at games and activities that are important to their classmates. They worry about their looks. They worry that they will do so well in school that they will antagonize their classmates, or so poorly that they will disgust them. They seek their teacher's approval but they certainly don't want to be known as a teacher's pet. They call each other on the phone to find out what to wear to school the next day. They are beset by inner pressures for peer acceptance, but they seek it by systematically weakening their own self-concept, even though people who are admired by others generally have a strong self-concept.

This anxiety for acceptance can result in various forms of (generally overt) misbehavior. In his zeal to gain the attention of his classmates, a pupil might engage in silly or exaggerated behavior. He may over-react to jokes told by classmates he wants to curry favor with. He may eagerly accept dares. Through all this he seeks to prove himself worthy of acceptance into the group he identifies with. If he is rejected by his classmates after all this effort, he may react by withdrawing completely, claiming total disinterest in his classmates and their interests.

Your challenge is to develop a spirit of acceptance within your room. Begin by exhibiting it yourself, by reinforcing behavior that builds your pupils' self-concepts, by working easily and graciously with each of your pupils in any grouping that might develop, by having pupils work together in many different groupings. There is certainly nothing wrong with pupils developing friendships and best friends, but you should work towards giving your pupils a maximum exposure to each other so that all will have plenty of opportunities to discover each other. For example, if you use room monitors, assign jobs by pairs. While two pupils who erase chalkboards together for a week won't necessarily become good friends because of the experience, procedures such as this that encourage constant interaction among pupils will help create an atmosphere that will give insecure pupils plenty of positive opportunities to be noticed by their classmates.

Instructional and teacher-related pressures also can create anxiety in pupils. Consider the following. Pupils who do poorly in basic reading and arithmetic skills fall farther behind as their classmates move ahead on these foundations. Many pupils become frustrated when their teachers don't clearly describe assignments and expectations. It's almost impossible for a teacher to hold the interest of an entire class at any given moment, so some pupils will always cut themselves out of the current activity and perhaps express their disinterest or boredom through misbehavior. Teachers have far more freedom of movement in a classroom than do pupils and this can cause tension between a teacher and active pupils who would like the same freedom. Most elementary teachers are women and they perceive the world through a woman's eyes, reinforcing behavior that is consistent with their values. That boys don't always share their perception of things is evident in that teachers more frequently punish boys than girls for misbehavior. Likewise, pupils who come from families who hold to values significantly different from their teacher's values frequently feel the pressures of conflicting values.

Note the diversity of pressures described above. It is perhaps because of this diversity that so much classroom misbehavior is directed against the teacher and the teacher's administration of the class. Studies that have been done in the area of classroom behavior seem to indicate that teachers are more apt to notice and react to misbehavior they consider deliberate and directed towards them. Such behavior is frequently disruptive and threatening to the smooth operation of the classroom. You can do much to reduce these pressures by handling such behavior properly. The next chapter will deal with this problem in greater detail.

Pressures That Affect Teachers

If the pressures ana anxieties that beset pupils can lead to misbehavior, then it's probably reasonable to assume that the pressures that affect you can also lead to misbehavior on your part. A teacher misbehaving? Really, it's nothing to be alarmed about. Misbehavior is fairly common in humans, and teachers are human. Whether we like to admit it or not, there are times when we act childish and annoy our pupils.

When you and your pupils explore the nature of the pressures that can lead to classroom misbehavior, include yourself in the study. Frankly examine the pressures of your job with them—not necessarily in an attempt to gain their sympathy, but rather in the spirit of helping them understand and appreciate the intricate complexities of classroom society.

We can identify three sets of pressures that affect a teacher in his work: (1) internal pressures, (2) pressures from people who interact with a teacher, and (3) institutional pressures.

Internal pressures are those you feel when you think about your job. Most teachers have a genuine concern for their pupils, regardless of what they might say in jest over coffee, and this sense of responsibility weighs heavily on them. You are responsible for preparing (in outline and in detail) the activities that will constitute the school day. You have the major responsibility for making the day a true learning experience for your pupils. You also have the responsibility for keeping things moving. Your pupils can tune out of things from time to time and relax, but you have to remain alert all the time (even though it's often next to impossible to remain awake while listening to a primary grade reading group on a warm spring afternoon). Mix into this need for constant alertness the pressures of personal problems, headaches, sleepless nights, a sick family, financial worries, a grueling drive to school—and it isn't strange that the pressures of being on top of the situation at all times can get to a teacher, and minor disturbances in the classroom can become major calamities to a teacher whose perception on a given day is temporarily distorted by pressure and anxiety.

It's a shame our pupils won't (or can't) tell us to go stand in the corner until we settle down. We could sometimes use it.

A second set of pressures arises out of *the interaction between teachers and other people* in their work. Even though you work with a good many other adults your contacts with them are somewhat fleeting—a word of greeting in a corridor, a request for something carried through a pupil messenger, a short chat in the faculty lounge, a comment via intercom, a preoccupied discussion while sharing playground duty with another teacher. Serious discussions on common professional concerns are infrequent, and then they are usually held after school when everyone is tired. This lack of complete and sustained communication with fellow staff members often results in misunderstandings that can lead to real tensions within a school staff.

The teacher misbehavior that results from this frequently

takes the form of an obvious coolness among teachers that is easily noticed by their pupils—constant negative comments about the pupils in another teacher's room, formal and forced conversation whenever the two teachers have to be together, hints and suggestions that the other teacher is somewhat deficient as a person and as a teacher. This is hardly the kind of behavior pupils should expect from those charged with demonstrating the dimensions of mature behavior.

Your contacts with your class are complete and sustained, but pressures can also arise here, though of a different kind. You work with thirty or so pupils and they all vie for your individual attention. Your plans to spend a few minutes working with a pupil who needs your help are frequently shattered by the insistent demands of other pupils who want more attention, explanations, and directions. The frustrations that build from these demands can be translated into various forms of teacher misbehavior—unnecessarily sharp retorts, general scolding of the entire class for the intrusions of a few, withdrawing of privileges, ignoring a child who really needs help.

Add to these pressures the pressures you sometimes face from administrators, custodians, secretaries, parents, pupils from other classrooms, neighbors, bus drivers, lunch room personnel, and others, and it becomes obvious that all too many people can intrude on your already crowded and busy world— and an all-too-human explosion can take place.

But when it does take place, should it fall on the shoulders of your pupils who might not have been directly or even indirectly responsible, and who can't understand why their teacher is so angry over the little thing that finally triggered the explosion?

Institutional pressures can also lead to frustration and misbehavior on the part of teachers. Facilities and equipment must be scheduled. All sorts of forms must be filled out. Films must frequently be ordered months in advance. Pencil sharpeners and projectors break down. The classroom must be arranged for the convenience of the custodial crew at the end of the day. Supplies run out. Lunch counts must be made. The intercom takes precedence over anything going on in the classroom. Class activities have to be scheduled around the schedules of special teachers and inter-class activities. Various non-teaching duties cut into the planning time teachers need.

The typical reaction of teachers to these pressures is to seek ways of getting around all the red tape that is such a burdensome part of their life. Supplies are stockpiled in the classroom against the inevitable day when orders for greater economies are sent down. Pupils are pressed into service to help keep records needed for the endless reports. Formal schedules are rearranged informally by teachers. Teachers cover for each other in assigned duties. Non-essential reports are turned in late, if at all possible.

Compare the bureaucratic pressures that annoy you with the bureaucratic problems your pupils face in your classroom. Any disturbing parallels? Can you eliminate rules and regulations in your classroom that are similar to the rules and regulations you chafe under?

UNDERSTAND THE NATURE OF MISBEHAVIOR

Misbehavior is generally defined as behavior that is inappropriate in a given situation—with someone other than the person whose behavior is in question determining what is appropriate and inappropriate in the situation.

Since most of us view our own behavior from a personal point of view, we tend to see our behavior as being generally appropriate. Consider the common classroom situation of a pupil not working on his arithmetic after the teacher had assigned it. The teacher considers such behavior misbehavior. The pupil might see it differently. He thinks, "I don't know how to work these problems correctly, and the teacher certainly doesn't want me to work them incorrectly—so I won't work them,"—or, "I already know how to work these problems. They're the same as yesterday's problems and I got all those correct, so why should I work these?"—or, "I don't feel like doing arithmetic right now. I'd rather finish this drawing first. I'll do these arithmetic problems this afternoon." Viewed from the pupil's point of view, his behavior isn't misbehavior at all. He thinks that if anyone is guilty of misbehavior, it's the teacher—for assigning work beyond his pupils' capacity in the first case, for assigning busy work in the second case, and for being too rigid about the use of time or for not adequately communicating the urgency of the assignment in the third case.

This suggests that the antagonism that often arises out of the handling of classroom misbehavior might stem from the conviction each party has that his behavior was appropriate and the other's inappropriate. A pupil is less apt to become angry about punishment if he agrees that he acted improperly, and a teacher should be less annoyed by negative reactions from pupils if he realizes that he's really not doing a good job of teaching. Unfortunately, things don't work out that way very often.

The pressures of classroom life described in the preceding pages contribute heavily to the one-sided view we generally have of the behavior of others. Classroom life is just too busy and complicated to permit participants to sit back calmly and reflect objectively about what is going on, to see things from the vantage point others have. Teachers and pupils alike tend to react to the immediate and differing pressures that are upon them, and the result is the classroom situation we all know only too well—the teacher with the single power to impose sanctions, and the pupils with the collective power to resist through devious methods. It's quite often a sort of stand-off.

Let's take a closer look at the varieties of misbehavior pupils and teachers are guilty of (in the eyes of the other) as they react to the pressures and tensions of classroom life.

STUDY THE VARIETIES OF MISBEHAVIOR

Hundreds and hundreds of research studies have delved into the behavior and misbehavior of pupils and teachers. Certain common threads seem to recur in these studies, and it is these threads that promise the most returns for a teacher who plans to explore classroom behavior with his pupils.

Pupil Misbehavior

While many classifications of pupil misbehavior have been suggested over the years, three sometimes overlapping general categories provide a simple and convenient arrangement of behaviors suitable for classroom exploration and discussion purposes: (1) disruption of classroom decorum, (2) behavior directed against the teacher and school, and (3) behavior directed against classmates.

Disruptions of classroom decorum are easily the most common form of pupil misbehavior. Individually, these somewhat minor forms of misbehavior do not disturb things unduly, but when they become a regular pattern of behavior in a classroom, they can become disruptive, and often seriously disruptive.

Disturbing noises lead the list. These would include talking, whispering, humming, coughing, sneezing, sniffing, and any number of other sounds the body can make. In addition, it would include the sounds pupils make when they drop books, sharpen pencils, crumble paper, tap pencils on desks, shuffle their feet, slam desk lids, and any number of other sounds we make when we come into contact with things.

On the one hand, it's difficult to understand why teachers get upset by noise. After all, what else could one reasonably expect from thirty youngsters who work together in a room where most of the surfaces are smooth and hard, and in a situation where communication is essential? On the other hand, it's next to impossible to work effectively with a room full of thirty youngsters when there is a constant undercurrent of noise that draws attention away from the activity the teacher wants pupils to focus on.

Herein is the dilemma, and here is where you can begin to explore the problem with your class. Some noise is inevitable, but too much noise is distracting. What can be done to resolve the problem? Explore a number of possible solutions with your pupils. For example, why not develop a science unit on sound that focuses on discovering ways of muffling as many potentially disturbing classroom sounds as possible? Or how about a study of the arrangement of the classroom furniture? Could furniture be arranged with sound bafflers as dividers between zones—thus permitting a certain amount of sound in one part of the room that would not be unduly distracting in other parts? Or how about a study of the day's schedule to see if quiet periods can be scheduled, so that activities that require quiet can be worked into the schedule with a minimum of trouble?

Disturbing movement is another kind of behavior that disrupts the decorum of a classroom. The more common forms of this behavior include aimless wandering about the room, taking the long way to get a drink of water or sharpen a pencil, running to the window to get a better view of something outside, and running in and out of the classroom. Another form of disturbing movement involves any unusual movement a pupil might make—rocking back and forth in his chair, slouching down in his chair, or waving his arm wildly to get attention during a discussion. A third form involves throwing objects such as wadded up paper across the room in an (often vain) attempt to hit the wastebasket, throwing paper airplanes and spitwads, tossing rather than handing books and objects to other pupils who have requested them.

Movement, like noisemaking, tends to draw the attention of pupils away from the activity the teacher wants attention focused on. Consequently, teachers are annoyed by it, and reprimand or punish pupils who do it repeatedly.

Here also, frank exploration with your pupils may reduce some of the problems that these behaviors can cause. Can the furniture be re-arranged so that pupil movement in the room is not unduly distracting? Chapter Five suggested a furniture arrangement that would actually reduce many of the problems identified above because the movement would not be visible to many of the pupils in the room.

Another question you might ask of yourself is whether or not you are unduly sensitive to movement. As a teacher, you are free to move about almost at will. What about your pupils? Is your school day so arranged that they are required to sit quietly for relatively long periods without adequate breaks? If so, your pupils might be trying to tell you something with all their movement. Even if you feel strongly that you don't want your pupils moving about the room without restraint whenever they want to, you could still schedule relatively frequent short breaks during which pupils could get up for a couple of minutes to stretch, throw paper in the wastebasket, turn in completed assignments, sharpen pencils, walk about, and discuss things with classmates across the room. Grant your pupils this and they might be willing to give you ten minutes of quiet desk-based activity between breaks.

Interruptions are another kind of behavior that disrupts the decorum of a classroom. These also take several different forms—pupils who interrupt you while you are busily engaged with another pupil, pupils who interrupt other pupils during a class discussion, and pupils who interject irrelevant topics into lessons or class discussions.

More often than not, a small group of pupils is responsible for most of the interruptions that occur during a given day. Consequently, the problem is a more limited one. Making general rules because of the actions of a few pupils can antagonize those who rarely interrupt. Making specific rules about interrupting for a few pupils makes them feel they are being discriminated against.

Constant interrupters want attention and/or they have a strong ego that is fulfilled through attention and participation. They often genuinely feel their needs are so important that you should drop all else and take care of them, or that their ideas are so good that they should be heard before anyone else's ideas.

While interrupters can be annoying, it's perhaps more important that you focus your attention on the reasons behind interruptions, and try to fill those needs, than it is to reprimand or punish pupils for interrupting. In the long run this should diminish the major sources of interruptions—and you should be able to live with the other interruptions that will occur. For example, if you notice that a pupil always seeks your attention when you are working individually with another pupil, it's possible that his behavior could stem from several causes, such as: he has a crush on you and is jealous of attention you give others; he receives little attention at home, and is fearful of losing the attention you give him at school; parental conflicts make him fearful of losing the love of those who care for him. Obviously, there is no simple solution to these or to any other problems that may lead to his interrupting behavior—but it's also probably true that a reprimand isn't the answer either. What is needed is your genuine concern, and your willingness to reassure him in as many ways as you can that you truly care for him that you are not forsaking him when you work with other pupils at times.

The kinds of misbehavior described in this section generally arise out of the tensions of thirty people living and working together, rather than from any dislike for a teacher or institution. Consequently, you should work together with your pupils in defining and establishing the limits for acceptable behavior within the class day. It just doesn't make sense for you to assume the full responsibility of lawmaker, prosecutor, judge, and policeman when dealing with these kinds of behaviors.

Behavior directed against the teacher and school is more difficult to deal with because criticism and hostility are implicit in these forms of misbehavior. The pupil's behavior itself is a message: "I don't like you, and I'm going to get even with you by annoying you."

Much of the behavior described in the preceding category could also be included in this category under certain circumstances. For example, suppose two pupils drop books on the floor. In one case it could be merely a matter of clumsiness —easy to deal with, laughed off with a humorous jest or a gentle comment about being more careful in the future. In the other case, the book could have been deliberately dropped to disrupt classroom proceedings—difficult to deal with, especially if the pupil follows with a feigned look of innocence all over his face.

Thus, in contrast to the preceding category of behavior, this category includes behavior that is deliberate, critical, and often hostile. It can be directed against the teacher, the school, rules and regulations, and/or any other aspect of "the establishment." It often takes the guise of relatively harmless forms of misbehavior, masked in innocence, but with enough edge to it so that the teacher gets the message: "Both of us know it was deliberate, but if you accuse me of acting deliberately, I'll complain loud and long that you're treating me unfairly."

Impertinence in its various forms is perhaps most difficult for teachers to take. "I won't do it." "You're a liar." "You can't make me." "Go jump in a lake." These and similar remarks, at times laced with profanity and obscenity and spat out within hearing of other pupils, place a teacher in a most difficult situation. The situation seems to call for an immediate response, but to respond immediately usually means to respond in anger.

Cheating is another type of misbehavior that often causes a dilemma in its treatment. When pupils cheat they attempt to deceitfully demonstrate a greater grasp of the material studied than they really have. Cheating is almost always deliberate, and it runs counter to long established standards of classroom conduct. On the other hand, the existence of cheating also frequently implies failure on the teacher's part—in communicating, in teaching, in establishing realistic standards of attainment, in evaluating. As with impertinence, cheating seems to call for an immediate response—but an immediate response made in anger may often be the wrong kind of response to make.

Some pupils deliberately use profane and obscene language and gestures to shock their teachers and to draw disruptive reactions from classmates. Such language is also used to punctuate otherwise mild forms of misbehavior, and thus give the behavior an immediate prominence it doesn't really deserve.

Another form of misbehavior directed against the teacher involves breaking specific classroom rules the teacher establishes, such as rules about gum chewing, running, leaving the classroom, and playing with objects when asked to listen quietly.

Vandalism is also a problem in many schools. Pupils write on the walls, mar furniture, break equipment, and break windows. Frequently such behavior signals deep-seated animosities against the school and/or specific staff members. It also suggests that the pupil feels little or no sense of ownership in the school. One doesn't usually deliberately destroy his own possessions.

It's very difficult to deal effectively with deliberately hostile behavior that is directed against you or the school, especially when it occurs within the sight and hearing of other pupils. Since the pupil often is baiting you with his behavior, you are wise if you don't succumb to the bait. If the behavior was meant to shock, remain unshocked. If the behavior was meant to anger, refuse to become angry. If the behavior was meant to force you to take a position, refuse to take a position at that time. In these situations, the pupil is attempting to establish the rules under which the disagreement will be resolved—often without clearly indicating what he is really angry about. It's best not to get emotionally involved until things are clearer, and tempers have cooled down.

It's also a good idea to deal with the show-downs these kinds of behavior imply out of the range of the other pupils. "Let's talk about that after school, George." "I'm sorry you feel that way, Mary. Let me think about it for awhile, and maybe we can talk about it later today or tomorrow." "I'm sorry you felt the need to copy your answers from Jane, Fred. Try to work them out by yourself now, and then later on we'll see how well you did on your own, and what your problem is with this."

Behavior directed against classmates generally has its beginnings in some action that took place prior to the disruptive action. An argument on the playground can erupt later in some classroom shoving. The lack of an invitation to a birthday party can lead to the snubbed pupil seeking reasons to tattle on the pupil with the birthday. It's important to know the circumstances that led to the disruptive behavior so you won't appear to take sides in the argument unwittingly by the manner in which you deal with the person who caused the specific disruption you have to deal with.

Fighting is perhaps the most common form of misbehavior directed against classmates. Physical fighting seems to be more common among boys and verbal sparring more common among girls, although neither sex really hesitates to use either form. Because of the explosive nature of fighting, it's important that you react rapidly to it. Determine at once whether the fight is between two pupils or two groups of pupils, or if a group of pupils is fighting one pupil. In any case, separate the fighters first. If possible, move them out of sight of each other, and preferably into isolation so that friends won't be available to keep fanning the flames of disagreement. Talk with each pupil separately and try to determine what happened. It's sometimes a good idea to delay these conversations for awhile until tempers have cooled. Try to bring the pupils together to settle their problems. Suggest some compromises and solutions to get things going. When the problem is solved—or a truce achieved—forget it. You will normally gain little by assessing punishments that might rekindle the anger.

Tattling is more difficult to deal with because the pupil who is tattling is pretending to help you in your work by calling attention to the misbehavior of others. Pupils who tattle either do not know or do not care that their behavior will only further antagonize their classmates, or else they feel their behavior will improve their relationship with you.

You probably shouldn't respond immediately to misbehavior reported by a tattler, and it's certainly not a good idea to respond in such a way that the tattler's classmates know that he called your attention to the misbehavior. Deal with such reported misbehavior quietly, doing nothing that will further antagonize the tattler's classmates.

Frankly discuss tattling with your pupils. It has within it some fascinating dilemmas that face man. Of course, what a pupil should do when he observes improper behavior in a classmate is to speak directly to the offender himself. The pupil's dilemma will occur when his remonstrations with his classmate are ineffective. Should he then forget the matter or come to you with it? There is no simple solution to this dilemma and your pupils should realize it. Policemen, diplomats, and cadets in service academies with honor codes face this dilemma every day. Some situations should be reported and some might be better forgotten. Discuss the issue with your pupils early in the year and try to define some basic realistic guidelines that are consistent with the pupils' codes of behavior. Then, when problems arise, re-examine and re-work your guidelines together and thus help your pupils grow in learning how to handle one of the thorny responsibilities of being a citizen in a democratic society.

It's really not unusual for elementary school pupils to become involved in sexual exploration. The lack of privacy and time in school limits these forms of behavior somewhat—primarily to telling obscene stories, sharing out-of-school experiences, and to some voyeurism and mutual feeling.

Over-reacting is a major danger in dealing with sexual misbehavior. Teachers are fearful of the stories that may go home if they do anything that can be remotely construed as condoning or accepting such behavior, so they tend to punish such transgressions severely, and at times even in full view of the entire class so there will be no misunderstanding about their views. If anything, the recent national furor over sex education in the schools has made teachers even more sensitive on this point.

Some pupils who become involved in sexually-oriented misbehavior are very embarrassed about the experience when caught at it, and others are somewhat boastful. In some cases, it's important to inform parents, and in others it might be better not to. As with impertinence, it's perhaps best to acknowledge the behavior immediately, but not to react to it immediately. Discuss the problem with the pupils after school or the next day, considering the specific nature of the behavior and its probable effect on the pupils involved. And then listen a lot during the discussion instead of spending your time preaching at them.

Teacher Misbehavior

Teacher misbehavior can be organized into four general categories: (1) poor preparation and teaching, (2) special relationships with pupils, (3) verbal abuse, and (4) unfair punishment.

Poor preparation and teaching are at the root of many classroom behavior problems teachers face. Pupils expect their teachers to be prepared and to do an adequate job of teaching, and they will react negatively when they discover otherwise. I was always confident my pupils would let me know by 10 A.M. when I wasn't properly prepared for the day.

Several problems relating to behavior arise when you are unprepared. It's difficult to give full attention to pupil reaction to a lesson if you are mentally planning the next lesson at the same time. The result is that you often don't notice potential behavior problems you would normally handle in stride until they become so serious that you have to halt everything and straighten things out. If you try to plan the next lesson during a short study period between lessons, you will be less able and willing to help pupils who need your help. You are apt to be curt in your responses when you do respond to their pleas, and talking and all sorts of fidgety behavior will begin as pupils look to their classmates for the help they expected to get from you. A third problem that arises out of a lack of preparation is that you tend to assign a lot of written work on days you are unprepared, and these assignments are often poorly conceived and inadequately communicated—mostly because you're not too sure yourself what you want them to do, except to keep busy. Such written assignments often imply long stretches of quiet seat work, which pupils don't like.

Another set of problems arising out of a lack of preparation involves materials and equipment. Consider the potential behavior problems in these situations: It's time to show a film or filmstrip and you have to stop everything while someone goes in search of the projector you forgot to get and set up earlier. You and your class arrive in the gym for P.E. and discover that another teacher had already checked out the balls, thus ruining the decision you made on the way to the gym to play Dodge Ball. You decide to run off some canned ditto master worksheets you just found for the next lesson while your pupils are occupied for a few minutes. When you get to the office you discover that the ditto machine is out of fluid and the secretary is in another part of the building. In each of these situations pupils will have to wait for a few minutes while you make on-the-spot adjustments in your plans, and in each of these situations you will probably become irked and take it out on your pupils in one way or another before long. If even a well-planned day has plenty of problems, why compound the difficulty by being unprepared?

The varieties of poor teaching that exist are matched only by the varieties of good teaching. In addition, what may be considered good teaching in one situation may be considered poor teaching in another. Pupils group much of what they consider poor teaching under the umbrella category, boring. A lesson is boring if it's beyond a pupil's capacity to understand, or if it deals with things he already knows. It's boring if it's directed at only a segment of the class and he's not in that segment. It's boring if the teacher doesn't keep the lesson moving, or if he moves it too rapidly. It's boring if the teacher isn't interested in the subject himself. It's boring if the teacher preaches at pupils. It's boring if the teacher doesn't give a good reason why the pupils should study the subject.

The traditional pupil response to a boring lesson is to turn the teacher off. Older students are generally kinder in that they usually only turn the teacher off mentally, pretending to listen. Younger pupils turn boring teachers off mentally, physically, and emotionally. They are also the most apt to add the ultimate insult—they'll leave the classroom in the middle of your lesson to go to the restroom.

Special relationships with pupils, whether positive or negative, can cause problems in a classroom.

It's probably true that more teachers are accused of having teacher's pets than are actually guilty of it. Nevertheless, such accusations rarely arise out of thin air, so if you hear such things about yourself, take a good look at your relations with your pupils. More often than not, a teacher's pet is a pupil whose values and life style are very similar to his teacher's. He sees in his teacher a good model for his own life. A teacher who notices this in a pupil is usually flattered by it, and often follows by trying to make a special impact on that pupil's life. Such a situation can be richly rewarding, with possibly a lasting impact on both teacher and pupil. There is nothing intrinsically wrong with a close supportive relationship between teacher and pupil. It's actually a good thing. It can be wrong, though, if such a relationship exists at the expense of the rest of the class (and this is what other pupils are often afraid of), or if one of the parties uses the close bond to take advantage of the other. It is never easy to deal objectively with a pupil who is also a good friend, but it is important that you do not let any such developing friendship become improper, too obvious, or unfair to the rest of the class.

Scapegoating is at the other end of the spectrum. If you find yourself thinking about and looking toward the same one or two pupils whenever something bad happens in the room, you are dangerously close to establishing a classroom scapegoat. What is so difficult about scapegoats is that they are actually often involved in the mischief for which they are blamed. What is so bad about a class scapegoat, however, is that he usually exists because the teacher covertly or overtly supports the scapegoating. The rest of the pupils are often only too happy to find a convenient set of shoulders upon which to place suspicions and blame that might otherwise come their way. And so the scapegoat gets blamed for everything, and frequently draws further and further into his shell as he sees no love and understanding coming in his direction. "I might just as well do what I want to do. I'm going to get blamed for anything that happens around here anyway."

Scapegoating is a sorry business for a teacher to be engaged in. If you have a scapegoat or the makings of a scapegoat in your room, give him the triple measure of your love and understanding that he desperately needs, whatever the nature and extent of his misdeeds. It shouldn't be any more difficult for you to forgive him than it will be for him to forgive you, and don't think that you don't need his forgiveness.

The seriously disturbed pupil may or may not fit in the above category. The very nature of his behavior demands that the two of you will have a close working relationship—whether you like it or not. If you have such a pupil in your class, you will have to take him into consideration whenever you plan any activity outside the normal routine of things—field trips, parties, joint activities with other classes, etc. And you'll have to stay close to him throughout the activity too. About the only sure thing in such a pupil's behavior is that his behavior is unpredictable, and often negative. The seriously disturbed pupil tends to place a damper on class experiences that could otherwise be enjoyable, because the teacher tends to tighten up and make more restrictive rules to account for that pupil's probable behavior. In addition, teachers eliminate some experiences they would otherwise schedule during the year because of the strong potential for trouble.

School life would be more pleasant if there was a simple solution to this problem. There isn't. As indicated in Chapter Six, you should involve available guidance and counseling services in your efforts to help such pupils, but much of the day-to-day work will still be yours. Accept such pupils as your charges, just as you accept those who are a delight to teach. Relax with them as much as you possibly can, and don't feel the need to make demands on them that are unreasonable *for them* in their present situation. You don't expect all your pupils to read equally well, do you? If you can relax, perhaps the rest of the class will too—and you may discover that even though such pupils' behavior is disturbing, it's not quite as disturbing as you thought it was. That's no solution to your problem, of course, but it's a beginning—and that's always where you have to start.

Verbal abuse can occur almost anytime—whenever a teacher has a headache, is tired, has had a family argument, is beset upon by bureaucratic machinery, doesn't know what to do next, has a stomach ache, is having trouble with pupils, or is bothered by a host of other factors that can stop things from running smoothly. At this point our voices get shriller, louder, more demanding, and often sarcastic. We say that we are scolding our pupils. They say we are hollering at them. A fifth grade pupil once told me that, "Whenever teachers get mad they start talking loud, then louder, and finally yelling. Then they start making mistakes when they talk, and then they get madder when we laugh at their mistakes."

It isn't always verbal. Another pupil comments that his teacher (who sat in the back of the room) "would become real quiet when she got angry, until you could feel her look coming through your back."

All of us are guilty of verbally abusing our pupils at one time or another—whether we rationalize our actions or not. It's such a common practice in schools that pupils have come to tolerate comments from their teachers that we wouldn't tolerate from others.

Listen to yourself and the language you use when you are angry. Be concerned if your pupils tolerate language that is essentially abusing and insulting. It could indicate that they're too used to hearing you speak that way—and that's not good.

Unfair punishment is a form of teacher misbehavior that can lead to many problems in a classroom. Pupils are willing to grant teachers a wide zone of tolerance in dealing with pupil misbehavior. They consider almost any disciplinary measure fair if it is administered fairly, or if they consider their teacher to be essentially a fair person. Pupils do react quite negatively, though, to disciplinary measures that are administered inconsistently, that don't arise out of the situation itself, that embarrass the pupil, that waste time with mere busy work, that make school work punishment, and that are excessive.

Pupils also resent punishment that is inflicted because of values the teacher considers important but they don't. Chief among these would be punishment for school work that is turned in late or that is untidy. Pupils wonder why an assignment has to be turned in at 10:30 A.M. when the teacher won't look at it until after school anyway. They wonder why they have to turn in assignments on time when their teacher often won't return it for several days. They wonder why they have to be neat and precise in their writing when the teacher's comments on their work is an illegible scrawl—difficult to read and interpret.

It might be a good idea to periodically ask your pupils to respond to a questionnaire that would probe your handling of pupil behavior. Do they consider you fair? Can they recall instances when you acted unfairly? What changes would they have you make?

In this chapter we have looked at the tensions and pressures that lead to conflict within a classroom and the nature of the misbehavior that results from these tensions and pressures. The next chapter will examine the responses teachers commonly make when they are faced with misbehavior within a classroom.

EIGHT

Responding Effectively

to Misbehavior

On any given school day you can expect to
deal with several dozen situations in which you are confronted
with pupil behavior that runs counter to the behavior you seek
in pupils.

You may decide to ignore a given situation or to react to it.
In either case, the decision will be based on your assessment of
the total situation. You might ignore a certain kind of behavior
in one situation and respond resolutely to similar behavior in
another situation. Within moments you may play arresting
officer, prosecutor, jury, and judge—and in many cases impose
the sentence before the defendant realizes that he has been ar-
rested, charged, and tried. It's all a most interesting facet of
classroom life, one well worth exploring with your pupils.

A teacher goes through three steps when confronted by

misbehavior: noting the misbehavior, determining how to respond, and responding.

NOTE MISBEHAVIOR

When teachers become annoyed at pupil behavior, they send out warning signals that pupils soon learn to read. Ask your pupils how they can tell when you are annoyed. Pupils' answers to this question are interesting and often revealing. They tend to fall into two general categories: a teacher either becomes louder or else suddenly quieter, and in both cases an intense stare usually accompanies the verbal behavior. In addition, pupils often also mention other physical movements or key phrases they associate with impending anger, such as pursing lips, moving towards a pupil, and tapping a pencil on the desk. Maybe it's a matter of survival for pupils, but they do become very adept at picking up the warning signals teachers (and parents) emit when they are annoyed.

I suppose I first discovered this during my initial year of teaching. One morning a sixth grade girl came up to me and said, "You're going to be grouchy in school today, aren't you?" I replied, somewhat surprised, that I really didn't know, but that I would be happy to consult my lesson plan book to see what my plans were. She continued, "We can tell because you're wearing *that* tie. Whenever you wear *that* tie, you're always grouchy." The other pupils standing around agreed—they all knew about *that* tie. They could even tell what days I had worn it in recent weeks.

I was thunderstruck. It was a flashy hand-painted tie in an ornate style popular then. Could it be true? Did I select clothes that fit my mood each morning? Did the gaudy tie appeal especially on mornings when I was tense, and therefore more apt to be irritable? It seemed unbelievable, but I took off the tie, cut it up, and threw the pieces into the wastebasket.

In retrospect, I wonder if I should have destroyed the tie. After all, it seemed to serve as a useful beacon to my pupils (and so it had a utilitarian value that far surpassed any other tie

I've ever owned). If my pupils were correct in their observations, the tie told them, "Watch out today. He's going to be touchy about things."

It's a good idea to help your pupils learn how to "read" your behavior as you react to their behavior. It gives them an opportunity to reconsider their behavior and to make adjustments, or else to prepare defenses before trouble begins. It keeps them even with you rather than always a step or two behind—and you'll discover, as did I, that it's an interesting topic to explore with your pupils. Some pupils seem to be in trouble much of the time, and this is frequently because they don't know how to "read" their teacher's emotional state. Their more perceptive classmates often do substantially the same things without incident because they have learned how to adjust their behavior to their teacher's moods—to misbehave at the right times, as it were.

Don't be afraid to admit that at least some of your irritation at misbehavior is dependent upon your current emotional state. It's a perfectly human response. If you see yourself and your pupils as human beings with human reactions, you're all apt to get along better with each other, despite the friction that will always exist in a classroom situation.

DETERMINE HOW TO RESPOND

You have two choices when you observe misbehavior. You can ignore it or you can react to it with some form of behavior control.

Much misbehavior that teachers normally react to would be better ignored—misbehavior that was accidental, that really doesn't disrupt anything important, that is essentially only another way of doing what was requested, that doesn't adversely affect anyone.

All too often teachers rebuke or otherwise discipline pupils for such behavior as: talking and moving about a bit while standing in line to get into the lunchroom (Have you ever watched a group of teachers waiting to go into a banquet hall at a conference?); making a contribution in a class discussion without asking permission at a time when no one else is seeking the floor (Why should a pupil raise his hand under those circumstances?); daydreaming instead of working (Daydreaming often is working for children).

If you decide to ignore a case of misbehavior, you also have to decide between informing your pupils that you are aware of the behavior but do not consider it offensive under the present conditions, or of just not letting on that you are aware of the behavior.

An example of the first situation might be when a rule against eating in the classroom is suspended when a pupil brings a birthday cake to school to share with his classmates, or if the entire class explodes and runs to the window when a house being moved down the street suddenly materializes at the window. Rare is the teacher who won't ignore propriety in such situations and join in the excitement. "Hey, you're not supposed to shout and run in the classroom, but I guess it's all right whenever a house drives down our street."

The second situation—of pretending not to notice misbehavior—is illustrated by the somewhat common situation in which a pupil who has been nothing but trouble all day long inadvertently misbehaves yet one more time at the end of the day. Why fight it? Tomorrow is another day—and hopefully a better one. The classic illustration of this second situation has always been, of course, that teachers should look the other way when a bully gets his comeuppance. (You might ponder that one.)

If you decide to react to misbehavior, the disciplinary technique you should use should be something that will stop the behavior immediately, but that will also help keep it from recurring. Consequently, the disciplinary measure should be addressed directly to the misbehavior. It should be the logical consequence of the behavior. Thus, a pupil who constantly bothers another pupil sitting next to him might be moved to another place in the room. In this case, the move is a direct consequence of the behavior and it should effectively stop the behavior for which it was imposed.

How permanently it will stop the behavior is another question. In the illustration above, it might stop the behavior permanently if it's just a matter of separating two pupils who were misplaced—who could get along with most of their classmates but not with each other. Such wrong combinations often turn up early in the year, and a few simple seating changes take care of most such problems for the rest of the year.

It does happen, though, that some pupils annoy almost anyone they sit near. Moving such a pupil would then have only temporary value. Its major benefit would be to provide relief for one group of pupils—probably at the expense of another group. What generally happens to such pupils is that they are eventually moved off to a corner of the room where they aren't near anyone else; and while this solves the group problem the class faces, it doesn't always get to the heart of the problem the individual annoying pupil faces.

Actually, many common disciplinary measures have little permanent effect on pupils. Nor are they really meant to be permanently effective. Teachers realize that developing self-discipline is the ultimate goal of all their work with pupil behavior, and that self-discipline is better achieved through a long series of gentle nudges than through a few dramatic pronouncements and blockbuster behavior controls.

It's somewhat similar to teaching language and arithmetic skills. Most teachers realize that these skills evolve out of much repeating and reteaching on their part—a lot of patience. They don't become unduly annoyed when pupils forget the words or number combinations taught yesterday. They quietly go through the material again with the knowledge that their pupils will eventually get it.

A teacher who is truly effective in classroom management does use behavior controls, but in doing so he skillfully and imaginatively selects and uses behavior controls that draw on three sets of contrasts: unpredictable/predictable, infrequent use/frequent use, severity/lack of severity.

Unpredictable/Predictable

Disciplinary measures that are a bit unpredicable seem to be more effective, because they do draw attention to the situation and they frequently examine the dynamics of the situation in a new way. On the other hand, predictable handling of pupil behavior has the value of giving the pupil an opportunity to weigh his behavior against the probable consequences of his behavior before he acts, and to decide whether or not it's worth it before he does it.

We could contrast these two approaches as follows. (Unpredictable): "You say you didn't work yesterday's arithmetic because you already know how to work all the problems, Billy? Well, show me. I'll give you a couple of the papers the others turned in. Correct them correctly and I'll agree with you and you can forget about the assignment. OK?" (Predictable): "Class, it's important that you do these arithmetic problems today because I'll need to know before tomorrow whether or not we can go on with the next topic. You'll have plenty of time to do this assignment during the rest of the day, but if any of you decide not to do it during school, you'll have to stay after school and do it. I'll be here until five o'clock."

Infrequent Use/Frequent Use

Infrequently used disciplinary measures, such as sending pupils to the principal, have a dramatic impact that frequently used measures never achieve. Pupils say of frequently used measures, "It happens so often that kids just think it's their turn to get scolded or something." "You're too used to them. They go in one ear and out the other." "Our teacher tries something new whenever the old things get worn out. Right now we have to write paragraphs whenever we do something wrong."

On the other hand, the continual use of gentle-nudge types of disciplinary measures, such as merely asking pupils to behave, seems to have a quietly positive effect in that these requests are more flexible in their intent and effect. "Let's have it a bit quieter in here." Pupils hearing this are placed into a position of having to interpret and change the present situation, as individuals and as a group, without specific standards being set. Such measures are frequently ineffective in the immediate situation, but they may be more effective in the long run in that they help pupils develop a sense of self-discipline.

Severity/Lack of Severity

There's no doubt but that the more severe disciplinary measures have a more immediate effect on controlling pupils' behavior, but there's also no doubt but that these measures can also create considerable antagonism in pupils. Consequently, the wise teacher limits his use of severe disciplinary measures to such situations as: when the situation is in danger of rapid deterioration if changes aren't made immediately, when other classes are being disturbed by the behavior, when danger is present, and when nothing else seems to have any effect.

A sixth grader commented on the tendency teachers have to begin with less severe and move towards more severe disciplinary measures as they deal with extended cases of misbehavior, "It sort of divides up the kids for the teacher. She won't do anything worse to those who obey, but she will to the others. They feel it's only fair to give everyone a first chance, even those who won't take advantage of it. If you just *ask* the good kids to behave and punish the others right away, it wouldn't be fair—so teachers do easy things on all the pupils first, then the things that work."

The poor teacher is more often than not characterized by pupils as one who is unable to make up his mind what to do, who really doesn't understand the situations that confront him. Such teachers frequently resort to idle threats in their indecision—and it is for such teachers that pupils reserve their most devastating ridicule: "I always wait until he says it's my last chance before deciding whether to quit. He always says when we have one more chance." "As long as she keeps pulling those 'one more chances' out of the bag, I don't have to worry."

RESPOND TO MISBEHAVIOR

Although teachers use dozens of different disciplinary measures to respond to misbehavior, most of these measures can be placed into six major categories: censure, removal, deprivation, referral, work, and corporal punishment.

Pupils become familiar with these categories of behavior control early in their schooling, and they soon come to expect that their teachers will use them singly and in combination to control class behavior. Thus, these categories serve a useful purpose in that they are accepted and understood by both teachers and pupils. They're comfortable, even though they're not always welcome or effective.

Explore these categories with your pupils in conjunction with social studies or health units, or as separate informal discussions and explorations. You may dicover a lot about yourself as you and your pupils take a close look at your reactions to their behavior.

Censure

The various forms of censure are the most frequently used and probably the least effective disciplinary measures in the teacher's behavior control arsenal.

Their popularity and general ineffectiveness both arise out of the way in which teachers commonly use them—as a first step in dealing with misbehavior. The mildest forms of censure —a simple request to behave, a pause, a glance in the pupil's direction, a quiet calling of his name—essentially serve notice to a pupil that you have noticed his behavior and don't approve of it. Thus, pupils often interpret these milder forms of censure as invitations to explain their behavior, rather than as demands to cease and desist immediately.

Since pupils generally do not consider their behavior to be misbehavior, they often will not completely stop their behavior after mild censure. Rather, they will tone it down a bit and emphasize any aspect of their behavior that might demonstrate the validity of what they are doing. For example, if a pupil is called down for talking with a classmate during a study period, he may look up and say, "I'm only showing him how to do these problems," and then continue on with much the same behavior as if his explanation took care of everything.

Because of this, it's better to observe carefully before reacting to misbehavior, and then to respond to what you assume to be the pupil's probable explanation for his behavior. "If you're going to help Bill with those problems, Kenneth, you'll have to do it more quietly. You're bothering others now." This kind of statement establishes limits for your pupils and gives them an opportunity to adjust their behavior without feeling a need to defend themselves from what they would consider a false accusation of misconduct. They are more apt to respond positively to a simple request under those conditions.

Much of the potential effectiveness of these mild forms of censure comes from the relationship you have developed with your pupils, since mild censure carries no real punishment with it. If your pupils like you and respect you, and if you are careful to be accurate and specific in your comments, you can do much to establish a wholesome non-frantic classroom environment through quiet comments and requests. Pupils prefer to work in such an environment and will do what they can to help establish and maintain it. Don't hope for perfection, though, because it doesn't work out that way. Too many different personalities and emotional cycles are involved in any classroom. Still, sincere purpose and constant effort can take you a long way, and the classroom environment you're striving for is remarkably more pleasant than the alternatives.

The non-emotional carefully modulated requests discussed above are only one step removed from the more severe forms of censure—scolding, threatening, giving an angry look, saying a pupil's name sharply, putting a pupil's name on a list. When mild censure doesn't accomplish what a teacher wants, he is apt to move up to these more severe froms of censure, assuming that these will bring about more immediate results. And he's right. They usually do.

Pupils do not see the severe forms of censure as invitations to explain and discuss behavior. The teacher is angry, no doubt about it, and he wants the behavior stopped immediately or else other forms of punishment will follow. Severe censure cuts off dialog.

The problem with scolding and other forms of severe censure is that teachers operate on a strictly emotional level when they scold. Consequently, they tend to make excessive statements and umbrella comments that berate the entire class for the misdeeds of a few. They threaten to do things they will be loath to carry out when pressed.

It's generally not a good idea to lose your temper in the classroom. It eliminates communication between you and your pupils since they don't even know how to respond to the situation. (Can they lose their tempers too?) It places you in a position of showing an immature side of your personality. And it can force you to make significant decisions under duress.

Nevertheless, there will be times when things go wrong. Your pupils will ignore what you consider simple and reasonable requests, and you will become increasingly annoyed by this on some days. Your voice will become shriller and you may say things you will later regret. Don't worry too much about it, though. Your pupils have been scolded before and they lived through it. When the smoke has cleared and everyone is quiet—deathly quiet—be big enough to apologize, and begin to pull together as a group once again, perhaps with a game or a song or a walk outside. "I'm sorry things got out of hand. It was just too noisy in here for us to do what we're supposed to do, and I guess I added to the noise too. Let's all go outside and cool off a bit. This morning I noticed a lot of discarded paper and other clutter in front of the school. Why don't we see if we can clean it all up in ten minutes or so?"

Removal

Quite frequently, the particular place a pupil occupies contributes to his misbehavior, and moving him elsewhere seems to be a good thing to do.

Several disciplinary measures hoary with tradition have evolved out of this situation—sending a pupil out into the hall, having him stand in the corner, or at the chalkboard with his nose inside a circle drawn there. These particular disciplinary measures seem to be dying out today, and a good thing it is too. I can recall once when one of my teachers had so many pupils standing in the corner that he established a waiting list. These disciplinary measures were used for all sorts of classroom transgressions, including not completing assigned work. How standing in a corner could speed up the completion of an uncompleted assignment was never clearly explained to me.

Moving a pupil can make a lot of sense if the place he presently occupies is a factor in the problem. For example, two pupils who obviously don't get along well should be moved to different parts of the room until they have learned how to get along with each other. A pupil with an annoying humming habit might be moved off to a corner where his humming won't annoy classmates so much. A pupil who needs a lot of individual help from you should be seated near where you tend to be much of the time. An easily distracted pupil should be moved to the front of the room where there are fewer visual distractions.

Simply moving a pupil to another part of the room may solve the immediate problem, but it often doesn't get to the heart of the real problem a pupil faces. Consequently, any such deliberate move implies a follow-up program that seeks to eliminate the need for such moves in the future.

Sending a pupil out into the hall is generally not a good thing to do. If a pupil can't behave in the classroom where you can observe him, it's difficult to see how his behavior can improve out in the hall where no one is observing him. I learned my lesson about sending such pupils out of the room unsupervised during my first year of teaching. The pupil wasn't there when I opened the door to let him back in, and I spent several anxious hours before he was discovered—slowly walking home. A teacher is responsible for his pupils at all times, and the last ones who should be let out of sight are the kind who typically get sent out into the hall. If you reach a point where you think it best for the tempers of all concerned that a pupil be removed temporarily from the classroom, take him down to the office or library (if someone is on duty there and if he likes to browse in books). If part of his problem is that he's tired, take him to the health room and let him rest for awhile.

In discussions with your pupils, you might explore the role of removal in larger society. Removal is a major factor in our society's punishment system. People such as thieves and murderers who demonstrate by their behavior that they can't get along with the rest of the population are removed from the greater society and placed into a more tightly controlled society of their own. Is this a good way to handle the problem? Does it stop the anti-social behavior and keep it from recurring? When prisoners are released and return into the general population, do they change their behavior? What is the relationship between the use of removal as a disciplinary measure in school and removal as a form of punishment in society?

There is a positive non-punishment side to removal. Policemen remove people from an area when danger is imminent to anyone remaining in that area. People are moved from one part of the country to another through job transfers. People move from one part of town to another if the move makes things more convenient. When pupils graduate from one school, the community removes them from that school and places them into another one. In some communities pupils are bussed to schools in other neighborhoods to promote racial balance in the community's schools.

Removal is more than standing in the corner. It's a fascinating social reality well worth exploring in its broader and narrower senses.

Deprivation

Deprivation can be a good thing. It often goads us to extra effort by making the thing we are deprived of increasingly desirable. If you see a coat you would like to have, you might do without other things in order to save the money you need to buy it. A college student might give up social evenings for school work prior to a vacation in order to complete assignments he would otherwise have to do during vacation. In both cases the anticipation—for a coat or for a vacation that is assignment free—goads the person on, and makes the goal an increasingly desirable one. Perhaps the illustration of enhancement-through-deprivation your pupils know best is the common practice of displaying wrapped Christmas presents for several days before they can be opened. Depriving the recipient of immediate knowledge of what's inside the attractively wrapped gift works his imagination and thereby enhances the entire experience.

Deprivation also has its bad side. Our society contains far too many hungry and homeless people who are deprived of basic needs that should be their birthright as human beings. These people differ from the people described above in that they are often deprived without being given a real option. It isn't a matter of doing without this to get that. It's a matter of doing without this *and* that. Extra effort wouldn't really solve the problem for many of these people either. Deprivation without choice or hope is wrong, and it's also a complex societal problem with no simple solution.

Deprivation has long been used as a disciplinary measure by teachers, sometimes with a choice and sometimes without. When a choice is involved, pupils will accept it. When deprivation is imposed after the fact, resentment is common. Contrast these two statements: (1) "We'll have science and art this afternoon. As soon as you are through with your science assignment, you can go to the table in the back of the room and start working with the clay. You should have plenty of time to do both, but don't dawdle with your science if you want to work with the clay," and, (2) "Too many of you dawdled over your science assignment this afternoon, so we just won't have time for art. I'm sorry, but it's your own fault." Both statements promise deprivation, but in the first case the teacher presented the options at the beginning when there was time to exercise either option, and in the second case the teacher announced the options after it was too late to exercise one of them.

Pupils will resent the second situation even though that teacher would insist that they should have realized that taking too much time for any activity automatically reduces the time available for subsequent activities. They will resent it because it's adult logic and not child logic, because those who didn't dawdle are being deprived of art with those who did, and because they will still insist that rules should be spelled out in advance.

Deprivation can be used effectively to help children develop self-discipline if choices are announced in advance and on an individual basis, if the choices are realistic and honest, and if the thing that is deprived grows out of the situation itself (and not, "Because you all were so noisy in arithmetic this morning, we won't have physical education this afternoon").

Occasionally it might become necessary to deprive a pupil of something after the fact. If a pupil brings a knife or some other potentially dangerous object to school, you might take it from him during the school day and return it after school. It's also a good idea to do the same thing with money or any other valuables if the pupil is displaying it carelessly. (It might also be prudent to check with parents on this.) But overall, the policy you should follow is that of outlining options your pupils have and the logical consequences of the various options they can exercise before depriving them of anything.

Referral

There are times when you may want to seek outside help in dealing with a behavior problem. Principals have historically filled this role, but counselors with specific assignments in this area are becoming more common in the elementary schools, and then teachers still involve parents when the situation seems to warrant it.

Involving someone from outside the classroom group can have the advantage of adding a touch of objectivity to the situation. This is particularly important if the pupil feels you greatly misjudge him and his behavior. This suggests that when you involve a principal or counselor you state the situation as accurately and clearly as you can, and then leave so that your colleague can further explore the situation with the pupil without your being present. You might feel that this procedure stacks the deck somewhat against you, but look at it from the pupil's perspective. He may see it that everything is stacked against him—two of you against only one of him. So let him speak freely, and even inaccurately. The truth will eventually come out, and through it all your colleague may well gain some understanding of your pupil's thinking you might otherwise never get—first hand or second hand.

In many respects, counselors are better to work with than principals because they lack the administrative authority of principals. They can only listen and suggest. They operate at the level of persuasion. This places them in a position where negotiation is necessary, and this is always a good thing when communication has been stifled sufficiently between participants so that help is needed to open it again.

Since teachers generally send pupils to the office only as a last resort, this action has taken on special significance in the oral traditions of pupils. "When you're in the first or second grade you hear about kids getting sent down to the principal's office and getting all mashed up, so you're scared when it happens to you." In many respects the worry of being sent to the office is as effective a deterrent to serious misbehavior as is the action itself—the awful walk to the office, the eternity of waiting outside the door, the remembrance of (exaggerated) stories told and retold by other pupils, the lump in the throat when explanations were sought. One pupil put it: "When I finally got there, I was really shivering but we had a nice talk. He really listened to what I said, and when everything was done I guess he said pretty much the same things my teacher had been saying, but I listened to him. I guess it's just because it was someone else saying it—and not that same old record playing over and over. I'll probably behave better from now on because I told him I would."

Teachers don't get together with parents over pupil behavior as often as they should. There is a tendency on the part of teachers to try to go it alone, and that's too bad because parents can be of substantial help in many cases. They're generally concerned about their child's behavior, and they know of facets of his behavior that teachers don't get to see during the school day. They are indispensable allies—if you get the information you need from them.

But that's the problem. Parents have become leery of the one-shot parent-teacher conference since such conferences typically weren't scheduled until things got really bad. The implication was always clear (to the parents anyway) that they were somehow remiss in raising their child. Consequently, they came in a defensive or argumentative mood, or else they came resigned to another in a long series of ego-shattering sessions—conditions hardly conducive to accomplishing much of a positive nature.

One good way to establish the positive information-sharing tone that gets you somewhere is to contact all your parents very early in the school year for information that will help you understand their child's behavior. Call them after the children are in bed, or send a brief questionnaire home. Ask about such things as: when their child goes to bed, whether or not he is expected to help around the house (and how he performs), what things tend to annoy him most, how he plays with brothers, sisters, and neighbors, if he tires easily, if he has problems with asthma, etc. If you thus clearly establish that you are only seeking information that will help you work more effectively with their child, you will most likely receive the kind of cooperation you want. More important, you will have established that you are sincerely interested in your pupils.

Follow this initial contact with a series of informal notes sent home or brief phone messages—comments jotted down in response to a child's behavior, and especially in response to the things the parents said about their child. "I notice that Billy's job of cleaning his room regularly seems to be paying dividends here. He always cooperates in helping keep our room clean. He tends to get tired (and sometimes irritable) in the middle of the afternoon. Could his 10 P.M. bedtime be pushed up a bit to see if that helps the situation? I'll report back in a couple of weeks. He generally plays well with others—he follows and leads as conditions suggest."

Such brief notes and/or phone calls during the first few weeks of the school year will help establish the relationship you will need when you get together with parents at the first formal parent-teacher conferences (probably at the first report period). You ought to be in a position at that time to discuss and expand on the information you have shared in a friendly and helpful manner during the early weeks of the school year.

If you can establish this kind of relationship with your parents, then you should be able to work effectively with them during the coming months when problems arise—and when the three of you need to work together to help the pupil, rather than to pull apart and hurt him. It's really worth every bit of effort it takes during the early weeks to establish this relationship.

Discuss the role of outside counselors in our society with your pupils. It's a broad spectrum of specialized occupations— tax consultants, marriage counselors, stock brokers, astrologers, ministers, "Dear Abbys," lawyers, and many others who keep more than busy advising others. Relate the need for these specialized roles in society to the need schools have for the various counselor roles they have established within the school society.

Work

Quite often teachers react to misbehavior by assigning work to pupils. The idea behind this is that if a pupil is occupied with some kind of work, he will be less inclined to engage in mischief. The work assigned is generally written work, such as writing sentences promising to behave, doing additional arithmetic problems, and copying pages from a book.

While it's not difficult to understand why a teacher driven to distraction by the behavior of a particular pupil might resort to almost anything to keep the pupil occupied, it's difficult to understand what positive results besides temporary relief can possibly come from make-work activities that have no more educational value than what the pupil was doing when he got into trouble. Writing "I will behave better from now on" fifty times will no more insure better behavior than writing "I will be a better teacher from now on" fifty times will insure improvement in teaching. In such classrooms the same pupils who were writing sentences in September are generally still writing them in May.

There are times when a pupil misbehaves mainly because he has nothing better to do. Your problem on such occasions is to get him interested in something positive rather than to substitute one form of negative behavior for another. "I know you're done with your arithmetic, Mary, but the others aren't. Why don't you go to the board and write a list of things you and the others who are done early might do while you're waiting for the rest of the class to finish." "I'm glad you have a few minutes, Bill. Would you be willing to arrange this set of pictures on the bulletin board so I can use them during our science lesson this afternoon?" "Frank, you're just the person I need—someone with a lot of energy. Would you run down to the office and get the filmstrip I ordered?" Many teachers have discovered that establishing interest centers, book corners, idea files, game boxes, and continuing art projects can do much to occupy pupils in constructive activities when they might otherwise misbehave.

Another form of work used as a disciplinary measure is that of requiring pupils to restore defaced or damaged areas and equipment—erasing marks and messages, filling in gouges, picking up litter, helping replace broken windows. Such disciplinary measures should arise directly out of the misbehavior itself. Perhaps more important is the curricular challenge vandalism raises; the amount of vandalism in a school is generally related to the sense of identity and/or ownership pupils feel in their school.

Corporal Punishment

While corporal punishment has an admittedly strong impact on the pupil and on the entire class, pupils generally consider it unfair. "It's horrible. Teachers just don't realize how it hurts your pride." "It's so embarrassing when the whole class watches you cry." "A teacher ought to be able to get kids to behave without shaking them and things like that."

Research studies dealing with pupil behavior consistently report that teachers rarely use corporal punishment, perhaps only about 2% of the time, and then it usually takes the form of something like forcibly moving or shaking a pupil rather than formal spanking. Some schools outlaw it completely. Nevertheless, corporal punishment has a dramatic impact far beyond its frequency of use, and herein lies the caution for its use. It's rarely a good idea to show anger when dealing with misbehavior, and teachers are generally quite angry when they resort to corporal punishment.

The simplistic solution to this dilemma is, of course, to stop misbehavior before it reaches the state where you and the pupil engage in hand-to-body combat. That corporal punishment can lead to other more serious problems is evident in this, that corporal punishment is the only disciplinary measure schools generally regulate by policy statements.

So, resist the temptation to engage in bodily combat, and instead focus your energies on mind-to-mind contact with your pupils. Spanking is easy. The mind is more difficult to get at, but it's infinitely more rewarding to reach in the long run.

And then, whoever said that working with a classroom full of growing youngsters would be easy?

NINE

Helping Children to

Develop Self-Discipline

*T*here is really no sense in working with children for years if they can't function responsibly by themselves in the end. An important goal of all formal education is to free students from the school's well-meant but generally unremitting control over learning and behavior.

This suggests that teachers and schools should progressively relax their hold over the behavior of pupils—within a given year, over the span of the school years—as pupils grow in self-discipline. Specific behavior restraints should not be placed on pupils beyond the moment when they are capable of acting responsibly in determining their own behavior in a given situation.

Examine the school year you are responsible for. What circumstances prevail with reference to your pupils and their behavior at the beginning of the year, during the middle months, and at the end? What can you do during the year you spend with your pupils to help them move significantly towards self-disciplined behavior?

Let's take a closer look at the special challenges each major segment of the school year presents, and see how solutions to these challenges can be drawn together into an effective program for developing self-discipline.

EXPLORE AT THE BEGINNING

The first month or so of the school year is critical in the development of positive classroom relationships because it is a time for getting acquainted—for forming first impressions and for discovering boundaries. It's a time when your pupils will observe you carefully because you are the key to much of what will happen to them during the year.

Respect your pupils' understanding of school society. Unless they're beginning school they will have had at least some firsthand experience in living and working together in a classroom. They have begun to realize that some restrictions on personal freedom are necessary in any social setting. They know that noise, movement, time, and space are variables that generally require some control. They know that you are assigned to their class as executive officer. And yet, with all these imposed restraints, they also believe that they have certain individual and group rights that no one can take away from them— by force or coercion.

Be straightforward with your pupils when you meet them during the first days. Define your role and their role as you and your community see it. Frankly tell your pupils how responsibility is apportioned in school—which decisions are their responsibility, which are your responsibility, which are shared responsibilities, and which are the responsibility of others beyond the class group. For example, playground schedules are developed by the school staff with the needs of the entire school in mind, and the teacher and pupils in an individual room cannot alter these schedules without the consent of the others.

The teacher and pupils in an individual room can determine, however, what they will do during playground periods—and while the teacher probably determines the order in which pupils will leave the room to go out to the playground, the two pupil captains of the teams determine the order in which their classmates are selected. So, decision-making operates at several levels.

Perhaps something should be said about the traditional advice that teachers should begin the school year with a show of authority, and then relax things in the weeks that follow if conditions warrant it.

This advice isn't completely without merit, especially if you are worried about the possibility of much disruptive behavior during the first few days—behavior that might arise out of a number of causes. For example, your pupils may have had an ineffective teacher last year; you may be moving into a totally new and unknown school situation; your school may have inadequate soundproofing between classrooms; or pupils in your school may follow a tradition of trying-out-the-teacher. In circumstances such as these you may decide to begin the year by establishing somewhat rigid and arbitrary controls over your pupils' behavior.

Beginning the year with a properly executed show of authority draws attention away from the individual personalities of the teacher and pupils, and instead focuses it on the total classroom or school situation itself through teacher imposed standards of behavior that are directed to the entire class group. No one is singled out. All pupils begin at the same place—at the bottom—with little opportunity for independent decision. With this approach pupils know where they stand. They know what's expected of them, and what will happen if they don't comply.

This approach also makes severe demands on the teacher, and so it gives pupils an excellent opportunity to see what kind of teacher they will live with during the next nine months. If you're going to demand the undivided attention and obedience of your pupils, you're going to have to reciprocate with some first-rate teaching. Without that, you won't be able to maintain the control you imposed at the beginning—and probably rightly so.

So beginning the year with a show of authority does have its advantages, and it does make sense in some situations. But it also makes special demands on you as a teacher, and it also delays the development of self-discipline in your pupils because they do not have to evaluate their behavior in ways that lead to self-discipline. Thus it's a mixed blessing. If at all possible, it's generally better to involve your pupils in the task of determining behavior standards and controls as early in the year as possible. The suggestions in the pages that follow will show you how to do this.

The early chapters in this book suggested many ways in which you and your pupils could study the relationships that exist within your classroom. From such study should come increased awareness of the dynamic and even volatile nature of classroom society. Try to identify early those major problem areas that will prevent your class from functioning effectively as a group, and then turn your attention to finding ways of solving these problems. Don't be concerned about instant success in the solution of your problems. Rather, establish an environment in which reasonable proposals will be heard and tried out. Your pupils need to be convinced that you are really more concerned with the long-range solution of their problems than you are with the immediate elimination of behavior that may be annoying to you.

Within the limits of *common sense* and *school policy,* seek ways to place your pupils into situations during these early weeks in which they will have opportunities to interact without your presence affecting their behavior. Go down to the office to get things you might otherwise send a pupil after. Send your pupils out to the playground or down to the lunchroom by themselves, telling them you'll be with them in a couple of minutes. Work off in a corner during tests. Note how your pupils react to these opportunities to act without the restraints of your presence. Then discuss these experiences with your class, focusing especially on individual responses to the situations. Does your presence dominate the classroom even when you're absent? Do tattlers and self-appointed group leaders arrange things so that one set of imposed controls is merely substituted for another? Do a few pupils so completely shatter the peace that the possible good behavior of the rest goes unnoticed?

Place individual pupils into positions of trust and discuss their reactions with them later. Let a pupil work by himself in the library for an extended period. Don't remind room monitors of their duties before they have had an opportunity to act on their own. Whenever possible ask pupils to arrange displays, set up equipment, keep records, distribute materials, and do anything else that will honestly place them in a position of carrying out a task with a certain amount of self-determination about the specific procedures they follow.

From the beginning focus your attention on rewarding positive behavior instead of on punishing negative behavior, even though you obviously will have to deal with negative behavior as it occurs. It's mostly a matter of emphasis. In general, reward is more effective in moving pupils towards positive behavior than punishment is. Punishment is liable to have emotional side-effects that confuse the learning situation. A pupil can't learn much about proper behavior while he's angry, frightened, or crying. Also, the punishment can cause aversive reactions to factors associated with the unwanted behavior that weren't meant to be included in the punishment. Scolding a pupil for spilling tempera paint you asked him to mix may remind him to be more careful in the future, but it may also lead to a lot of resentment over being embarrassed by your scolding—and so what you've done is to substitute one problem for another.

Do what you can to reinforce any success your pupils have in coping with the self-discipline challenges you present them. Rewards needn't be elaborate, and some of the best come out of the situation itself. A smile, a pat on the back, or a favorable comment are common. But even when you return to an orderly room without comment, you can reinforce positive behavior if your whole bearing suggests that this is precisely what you would expect from your class.

Comments such as the following are important to pupils because they emphasize the confidence you have in them and in their ability to function independently: "Thanks, Sally. Would you do it again tomorrow?" "Fred, can you fix this so that it doesn't wiggle?" "You looked so interested in what you were writing, Tom, that I can hardly wait to read it." "Would you three girls set up the volleyball net again today? The rest of us will be down in a few minutes."

The manner in which you distribute rewards and reinforcements can affect your pupils' development of self-discipline. The simplest way, of course, is to reward every acceptable behavior your pupils demonstrate. Research has indicated, though, that this isn't necessary to maintain performance; that a random schedule of reward actually seems to be a more effective schedule in many situations.

The slot machine is a good example of a random schedule of rewards. It pays off on a fixed schedule, perhaps one out of ten tries, but on one occasion it might pay off twice in a row and on another occasion only once in twenty tries. The general popularity of various forms of gambling attests to the acceptance this reinforcement schedule has.

We can see random schedules operating at other levels too, and these help support the development of self-discipline. Consider how we prize the unexpected word of commendation, the unsolicited testimonial. Such rewards can make our day and keep us working productively for a long time between rewards.

Different people operate on different schedules. A pupil who has achieved success may be able to work effectively for a long time between rewards, while a pupil who is rarely successful might need to be reinforced every time he does something right in order to keep him going.

This suggests that, while you can relax when you deal with children—free from the need to feel that you have to react to everything positive they do—you should still study your pupils intensely to discover how well they are moving towards self-discipline.

The early weeks of the school year are, then, a time to study and a time to try out, a time to be thrilled when things go right and a time to shrug off minor failures when they occur. It's a time for faith in the capacity of children to mature. Things will never improve unless we truly believe they will, and unless we're willing to give our pupils a genuine opportunity to work out their own problems.

GROW DURING THE MIDDLE MONTHS

There comes a day when the beginning of the school year is over and things settle down to a routine. This is the period when the year's major accomplishments in learning and class relationships usually occur. This is also a period when you should involve your pupils more in the decisions you tended to make on your own at the beginning of the year before the group was cohesive enough to act effectively.

Perhaps the best example of this involves the procedure and behavior rules you established at the beginning of the year. As indicated earlier, many teachers impose somewhat stringent rules at the beginning of the year on the assumption that if changes have to be made it's easier to relax stringent rules than it is to tighten lenient ones.

As soon as things settle down and your class is able to begin to examine its own individual and collective behavior, they should take a good look at the rules you established. Work with your pupils as they suggest modifications, deletions, and additions, and then see how things go. If a change doesn't work out try something else until your pupils discover how they can best live with each other and with the other people who share the school facilities with them. Don't worry unduly that it might take awhile to discover this. Reading and the multiplication tables take awhile to master too, and learning to determine one's own behavior is at least as important as mastering those skills.

Continue this self-evaluation through the year. You may be surprised to discover how much children can mature in assuming responsibility for their behavior if they are honestly involved in making decisions, and if they are held accountable for the decisions they make.

While you and your pupils may focus your attention initially on behavior and procedures that are essentially routine in nature—procedures for sharpening pencils, going to the restroom, handing in papers, etc.—you should move on to more significant problems in classroom life, problems that help a group confront itself unexpectedly in new and different relationships. What would we do if someone suddenly became sick to his stomach? What if a bee flew into the classroom? How will we react when a new pupil is enrolled in our class? The list of possible behavior situations is endless, and so it's really not advisable to focus on every specific situation that may come up.

A better approach is to define types of situations that might occur and discuss individual and group responsibilities in such general situations. For example, the bee intrusion mentioned above is one of literally dozens of similar more specific threatening intrusions from outside the group, ranging from noise in the corridor outside the classroom to threats from bullies to "get" pupils on the way home from school. Chapter Seven dealt in detail with major kinds of behavior disruptions that can affect a class group, and you could work with these categories in your studies (either in formal health and social studies units on school relationships, or in a series of informal discussions you schedule during the year).

In addition to class discussions (and role playing sessions) that deal with problems before they occur, be willing to stop everything and evaluate behavior after something has occurred. One good way to do this—if it's possible—is to have a tape recorder easily available at all times in your classroom. Then whenever anything occurs that is bound to cause varying pupil reaction, turn on the tape recorder and record the situation as it develops. When the situation has resolved itself, replay the tape and discuss the reactions your pupils exhibited. In such discussions be slow to criticize. Instead, concentrate your attention on analyzing the situation with your pupils. What happened? How did it happen? Did the behavior lead to further problems or to the resolution of the problem?

As you move through the year encourage your pupils to note and report on examples of self-disciplined behavior in the newspapers and in their daily lives. Don't look for the spectacular. The pupil who went out of his way to deposit a candy bar wrapper in the wastebasket can be an excellent example. Discuss such situations with your class as your pupils report them. Your class might even want to send notes of commendation from time to time when they notice schoolmates, teachers, custodians, and others going beyond the requirements of the job or situation to demonstrate a special concern for the well-being of others. Contrast such behavior with the rudeness and inconsiderate behavior your pupils also see in society and your pupils will begin to understand the significance of developing self-discipline in citizens in a democratic society.

Arrange things so that you can observe the behavior of your pupils as individuals. One way of doing this is to focus your attention on a single pupil each day. On that day work things out so that pupil has many opportunities to interact with his classmates and to react to decision-making situations with a minimum of direction on your part. After school jot down your reactions to his day. During the year you should observe each pupil about six times in this fashion, and these records should give you a good sequential account of the pupil's development in this area throughout the year.

Find a few minutes each day to discuss yesterday with the pupil you observed, and when you have made the last such observation of a pupil during the year, make a special effort to recap the growth you noted during the year.

Although student government will probably never really be a major force in the operation of elementary schools, it can certainly become much more significant in the educational development of children than it generally is today. What is most often wrong with class and school-wide student government at any level is that the teachers and administrators really don't trust the students with any decisions beyond the trivial. They are fearful the students will make "wrong" decisions, oblivious of the fact that it is rare that any adult governing group makes a decision that is universally applauded as "right."

It would seem logical that the only way citizens in a democratic society can really learn how to govern themselves is to govern themselves, and that means making and living with both right and wrong decisions during the learning process. Schools should systematically involve their students in decision-making at a level of responsibility consistent with their development in the skills of governance. The student governments of many colleges and universities today are demanding control over the spending of student incidental fees funds that often run into the hundreds of thousands of dollars annually. What school-based preparation have they had for such responsibility?

The preparation of responsible student governance must begin in the elementary school. Begin by defining areas of real responsibility that you can properly turn over to your pupils, and then let them *really* make the decisions. Be willing to live with whatever decisions they make in those areas. If they make a wrong decision, let them discover it and try to correct it without undue meddling on your part. When the entire sequence of decisions has run its course, and your pupils are satisfied with their final decision, then you should step in and help them go over the discussions they had and the decisions they made as they worked through the problem.

What kinds of decisions can you turn completely over to the pupils in an elementary school class? You are pretty much limited to things that essentially involve them and their interests alone—things that do not affect other teachers or classes. At its most uncomplicated level this would involve decisions that relate perhaps to such things as planning class parties and deciding who gets to use what during recess. A second level of decision might include such issues as classroom seating arrangements and behavior. A third level might involve making decisions about such things as the group's relationship to some non-class group or activity (such as an all-school event). In every case, you do have a responsibility to help your class define the limits of its decision-making power—to weigh such factors as safety, legal considerations, individual rights, etc.

Explore various organizational schemes for decision-making with your class during the year. You might want to begin simply, with a town hall arrangement that requires only a chairman and secretary. Later, you may want to explore the use of committees, delegate assemblies, and the like. What advantages and disadvantages does each system have? Which is the most efficient? Which comes closest to representing the will of the group in its decisions? Encourage your pupils to discuss the processes they used to arrive at the decisions they made. Change your student government organization several times during the year, perhaps every six weeks or so. This will enable more pupils to assume leadership roles, and it creates more opportunities to try innovative ideas.

Take the lead in encouraging the development of a school-wide student government that is really given an opportunity to address itself to issues and problems that affect all the pupils in your school.

As your pupils become more and more involved in real self-governance, their attitude towards the school should become more positive. People who are really involved in the operation of an institution are the institution. Rebellion only comes from those who do not participate in the decision-making process of an institution, or whose participation is seriously curtailed by those in charge.

A sense of humor is especially critical during the middle months of the school year when the novelty of the beginning has worn off and the end seems such a long way off. There will be days when you take yourself too seriously, when the minor frustrations of life take on added importance, when you consider your own well-being more important than anything else, when you despair of ever teaching your pupils anything. If you have done right by your pupils in developing an open and supportive classroom atmosphere, they will most certainly take care of you on such occasions, bringing you back to reality with a quip or remark like, "How come you're so touchy today?" Take it for what it really is—a kind way of asking you to show the self-disciplined maturity they know deep down you possess.

EVALUATE TOWARD THE END

The final weeks of the school year are a time for reflection and summary. Don't waste this important time in a frantic rushing about to complete textbooks and units and courses of study. Relax. Live a little with your class. Take plenty of time to think and talk about what has happened and why it has happened—the good and the bad.

Spring is a pleasant time of the year, a good time to get off by yourself as a group. Walk together to a nearby park and sit on the grass and talk. Go to an art museum and observe how various artists interpret a world your pupils are also discovering. Walk around in the business district and note together how rules shape people and how people shape rules. Watch a family of birds build its nest. Walk down a nearby street and see how much litter you all can collect—litter that really shouldn't be there. Plant flowers that someone else will enjoy after the school year is over. Ask an older couple in the neighborhood to spend a day with your class—giving of your youth, drawing on their age. Capitalize on every opportunity you have to move your pupils' vision beyond the confines of your classroom into the larger world. Discover and discuss how the two worlds are similar and how they are different. It is from these discoveries that your pupils will see relevancy or irrelevancy in formal education.

Grant more real freedom to your class during these last days—traditionally a time when teachers tighten their control over class behavior. If you have spent the year doing what this book has suggested—making the school itself the proper study of the school—you should have little to fear. It's true that your pupils still may make more noise than you want them to make, that they may still argue with you and with each other, and that they may still neglect your assignments in favor of their interests —but would bearing down on them really change the situation?

Probably not. So act and evaluate as you have all year. It's far better to end the year hard at work trying to solve the interpersonal behavior problems you and your pupils have faced all year, and that your pupils will continue to face throughout life than it is to bear down and to create a situation that pretends that interpersonal problems can be eliminated if only one imposes strong enough controls from above. Seek self-disciplined behavior in your pupils if you truly believe in the existence of self-discipline.

Spring is a time for new life and new hope, and so it's a delightful time in which to end the school year. It's a time to have hatched, to have sown—to say goodby with no regrets. It's a time to look forward to three summer months in which you can savor successes and forget failures. It's a time to know deep within the recesses of your soul that your experiences with this year's class are bound to make you a better teacher next fall when you start all over again with another group.

Index

A

A.A.A.S. elementary science program, 127–128

Accuracy and *precision*, differences between, 135

Achievement tests, examining for proper interpretation, 97–98

Actions, communication of values through, 48–51

Adler, Irving, 126–127

Adult society, responsible, projecting in your classroom, 57–74
  expectations of society, 58–59
  problem areas, 59–67
    patriotism, 63–65
    politics, 62–63
    propriety, 65–67
    religion, 60–61
  pupils, aiding their understanding of you, 71–74
    first days, 71–74
    throughout year, 74
  self-examination, 67–71
    annoyances in classroom, 69–70
    regarding people with whom you work, 70–71
    pressures of classroom life, 67–69

Advertisements, newspaper, as indicative of value variability, 41

All the pupils, getting to know, 87–91

Annoyances in classroom, self-examination about, 69–70

Apathetic teachers more of a problem than partisan teachers, 63

Arithmetic as search for simpler way to communicate quantity, concept of, 122

Art as celebration of · ordinary, teaching concept of, 121–122

Authority, particular show of in first few months of year, 193–194

B

Beginning of school year and consideration of self-discipline, 192–197

Behavior control, categories of, 178–189
  censure, 178–180
  corporal punishment, 189
  deprivation, 183–184
  referral, 184–187
  removal, 181–182
  work, 187–189

Behavior problems, special, seeking help for, 91–93
  behavior diaries, 92

"Black Box" as game to teach children inferences, 132–133

Body as basis for person's beliefs and values, 41–51
  through actions, 48–51
  through language, 45–48
    songs, 47
  through skin, 41–45

"Boring" as "umbrella" category for all things unpleasant, 165

Bruner, Jerome, 119–120

Bulletin board display as introductory device for teacher, 72–73

C

Carrels for privacy and individuality for students, 102–105